THE MIND-CHANGING HABIT OF JOURNALING

The Path To Forgive Yourself For Not Knowing What You Didn't Know Before You Learned It - A Guided Journal for Self-Exploration and Emotional Healing

ZOE MCKEY

For general information on the products and services or to obtain technical support, please contact the author.

Contents

Free Gift Alert vii
Free Gift Alert II xi
Introduction xiii
Before You Get Started xxix

1. Step One: Awareness 1
Journal Mode 27
Complimentary Journal for Chapter 1: 33
2. Step Two: Stop the Blame Game 62
Journal Mode 89
Complimentary Journal for Chapter 2: 103
Untitled 105
3. Step Three: Forged in Pain 135
Journal Mode 157
Complimentary Journal for Chapter 3: 175
4. Step Four: Conscious Transformation 196

Journal Mode 209
Complimentary Journal for Chapter 4: 215
My Ideal Self 219
My Healing Fantasy 221
My Role Self 225
Final Words 229
Are You Still With Me? 233
Other Books by Zoe McKey 237
References 243
Notes 247

Free Gift Alert

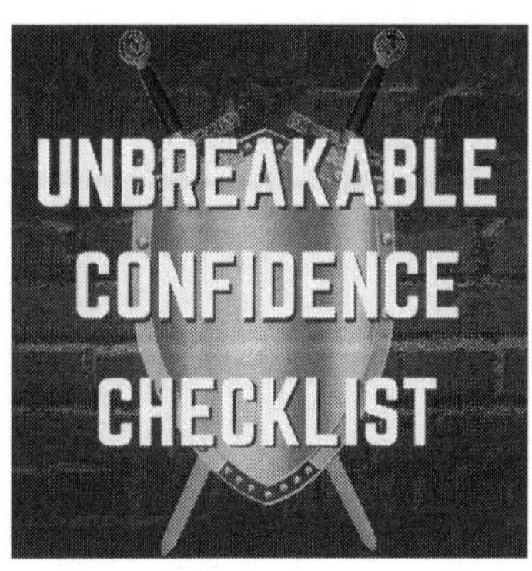

Thank you for choosing my book! I would like to show my appreciation for the trust you've given me by offering you **FREE GIFTS**!

To download your FREE GIFTS visit www.zoemckey.com.

The checklist talks about *5 key elements of building self-confidence* and contains extra actionable worksheets with practice exercises for deeper learning.

Learn how to:

- Solve 80% of your self-esteem issues with one simple change;
- Maintain your confidence permanently without falling back to self-doubt;

- Not fall into the trap of promising words;
- Overcome anxiety; and
- Be confident among other people

The cheat sheet teaches you three key daily routine techniques to become more productive, have less stress in your life, and be more well-balanced. It also has a step-by-step sample sheet that you can fill in with your daily routines.

Discover how to:

- Overcome procrastination following 8 simple steps;
- Become more organized;
- Design your yearly, monthly, weekly and daily tasks in the most productive way; and
- 3 easy tricks to 'level up' your mornings

Visit www.zoemckey.com and download your FREE GIFTS now!

Free Gift Alert II

What? Another one?

That's correct! I know that stepping on the journaling road is difficult so I'd like to make it as easy for you as possible. This book follows a unique journaling method, as you'll soon see.

My hope with this printable journal is to help you complete the exercises as you progress with your reading. I added the full complimentary journal section to each chapter's Journal Mode in case you hate printing. But my pro tip for you is to download the printable journal as soon as you get to the part in the book where you'll find the link to it as you'll have much more space to elaborate on your thoughts.

Take out your colored pencils or your black ink and start jotting your thoughts on those papers. Doodle, color, and get deep inside your head. And most importantly, be honest.

Introduction

In November I got a therapist.

Done. It's out there. It's official. You may think, "I have one too, it's not a big deal." You're right. In the United States and many other developed countries, having a therapist is nothing special. In fact, many people have multiple therapists, one for each issue they are facing; a therapist for their anxiety, a relationship therapist, a therapist for their dog... But in Romania and Hungary, I tell you my friend, when you confess you have a therapist (a psychologist, as we call it), people instantly take two steps away from you, slow their speaking speed as if they were talking to a three-year-old and ask you with a condescending and worried face, “Are you okay?” (Try to read this sentence with your best talking-to-a-dummy voice.)

Okay, I’m half kidding. Some people in my home countries are quite open-minded about having a therapist; some even have one just like I do. But it’s true that the majority of people will stigmatize you for it. Or, at least, that’s what everybody is thinking. So hardly anybody confesses that they have a therapist, and as a consequence this outrageous afternoon activity still remains a taboo in conventional Eastern European thinking; people who seek out a therapist must be c-r-a-z-y, period—and the catch-22 persists. I have this conspiracy theory that everyone has a therapist in Hungomania (as I call Hungary and Romania) but nobody knows about it.

We are all crazy, come on. Some of us just have special seasoning to it. And when I say crazy, I don’t mean it in an offensive way. I mean that all of us have issues—some bigger, some smaller—that we should talk about with objective outsiders. When we only recycle our problems in our own mind, we won’t find a solution to them. Why? Because if there was a solution to that particular problem within us, it probably wouldn’t be a problem anymore.

Others can see us—our behavior, our habits and our struggles—with much more clarity than we do. Whether we like it or not, our mind is susceptible to biases, can be overwhelmed by emotions and can deny real problems for the sake of the safety of the status quo which are not exactly the factors a good solution needs.

A very common excuse to not have a therapist is, "But I share my issues with my friends and family." Yes, I was totally guilty of this kind of thinking as well. I was also cheap about it: "I won't pay the big bucks to someone who doesn't care to listen to me whinge for an hour. They get to go back to their twisted life. If they were okay, why would they become a psychologist in the first place?"

I'm not proud of my excuses. This is another popular piece of propaganda against psychologists in Hungomania: if someone takes psychology as their major, it is for the sole purpose of fixing themselves. And... what's wrong with that? What's wrong with being so self-aware at the age of 18 to deliberately choose to address your 'childhood pack'? Heck, I wish I got the sense at that age to pull my shit together and discover all the things I will talk about in this book. I waited an extra decade to 'fix myself'. And let me tell you something, the behavior flaws the world forgives at the age of 18... it won't forgive them at the age of 28, 38 and so on. What at the age of 18 comes off as 'immature but lovable' or 'a bit of a rebel' at the age of 28 comes off as 'irresponsible, childish and unacceptable'.

Our unhealed past will get back to us over and over again, causing conflicts around us, pushing us towards present-tense misery; and the worst part, we won't even know why... I don't know about you but I was totally oblivious about the things I had been doing wrong on a day-to-day basis. To me, whatever I did was 'normal'. "This is how I've been all my life," I said to myself—sometimes defensively, sometimes proudly. I wish a more adult side of me would have pulled me away during those times and shook the soul out of me shouting, "And you think that's good; that you act the same immature way as when you were 16?"

Maybe I'm the only childish one out there and everyone else has 'figured themselves out already'. But another hard lesson I learned recently is that I'm not so freaking special. Whatever I think my personal problem is, if I put it into Reddit's search engine, I can read another 247 people raging about the very same thing. Incredible! And yet not so much. While my specialty-driven ego is devastated, my real self is extremely grateful and happy that I'm not alone with my problems and I can contact any stranger in the world through an application and share our pain and heal together.

Here is the thing about strangers: they don't know you, so they are less connected emotionally. Therefore the chance that you'll get an honest evaluation about yourself is higher. And on the pedestal of honest strangers stands the therapist, as I learned in my self-discovery journey.

Who do you tell your problems to? Your momma, who (hopefully) sees you as the most perfect, precious star that has ever shone in her sky? Your friends, who may or may not be gutsy enough to tell you something hurtful? Don't get me wrong, it is awesome if you can talk your problems through with your friends and family, but they may not give you the answers you *need.* A therapist doesn't know you —isn't emotionally attached to you—and if you choose a good one, has a lot of experience and education behind them and knows how to ask meaningful questions and point out crucial errors in behavior and thinking.

My therapist, Andrea, does just that. She is one of the most non-judgmental human beings I have ever met. I remember the very first occasion we spoke I told her matter-of-factly, "Look, I'm not crazy." She just nodded. I waited for a few seconds. *Maybe she'll react somehow now.* Maybe she'll tell me that this is exactly what a crazy person would say. Maybe she'll tell me sorry, she can't treat me, and the next moment two huge gorillas would enter carrying a medium-sized straitjacket and drag me away.

I sunk into this whirlpool of fears; that my mother has schizophrenia, that my country would stigmatize me, that I'm weak and I self-admittedly can't keep my stuff together. In the meantime Andrea just sat there, waiting for me to come back from my irrational land of fear. All this happened within a matter of seconds. When I saw that she didn't have a disapproving comment on what I had just said and no gorillas appeared, I cleared my throat. "Right," I said. And then I burst all my aforementioned fears out to her.

She told me that having these fears is normal and that, in fact, more people have it than I would imagine.

I'm not the only one who has issues? This simple realization worked like magic on me. I'm not the only one. I'm not alone.

I write self-help books and I tell my readers things like "You're not the only one." and "Your case is not that unique." I say these things because I can empathize with you. But it never occurred to me that you could also empathize with me—that we share a common humanity that goes both ways. When you are the one who provides understanding to others, sometimes you forget to seek understanding for yourself.

In my opinion, that's what a therapist is for. They will give you understanding and also help you better understand yourself. If you, my reader, feel that you listen to others but you hardly ever feel listened to, this book is for you.

This book is not about the perks of having a therapist, though. This book is about one particular perk of having a therapist, one of their recommendations, which doesn't necessarily require a therapist to fulfill. This advice is to **keep a journal**.

I'm fairly sure you're familiar with the activity and

you may roll your eyes just like I did when Andrea first told me I should try doing it. *Really? That's why I'm paying you?* I thought. *Is this the go-to plan? Writing my thoughts on a piece of paper? Didn't we just agree that my thoughts are flawed and recycling them wouldn't lead me to a solution?*

I was skeptical. I convinced myself to get a therapist for the very reason I first convinced myself that I shouldn't think alone: because my thoughts about my life are biased, overwhelmed by emotions and full of denial. And now she's telling me to go back to ground zero and do exactly what I'm trying to escape? Think about my thoughts. *Journaling. What a joke.*

But what if my instant disinclination towards having a journal roots in my biased and full-of-denial, (ir)rationalizing mind? What if my resistance is exactly what I tried to escape first by getting a therapist, second by not listening to that therapist? What if I needed to go through this since by myself, the Lord as my witness, I would have never sat down to write anything about my thoughts?

I got up and went to the paper store to pick a journal. Browsing through the booklets of all shapes, sizes and price ranges, my eye stuck on a pile that had bunnies on their cover. They were very cheap booklets, not even a dollar each. I took a closer look (as I love bunnies) and read the headline on the first page: *A Noteworthy Thought... Come on, seriously?* I felt slightly pissed. If you are a long-term reader of mine, you may already know my natural disdain for spiritual ideas such as the law of attraction. But in that moment, I kid you not, all I could think of was, *this is a sign, I attracted this booklet.*

When I realized what I just thought I almost ran out of the shop, screaming, "I AM crazy!" In the next moment, however, I picked up three of the bunny booklets, went to the cashier, and with a huge blush, as if I were trying to purchase three XL-sized condom packs, I paid.

Phew. I went back to the safety of my home and quickly read one of Mark Manson's sarcastic articles on self-deception to cleanse myself from the brief 'law of attraction is real' thought. *Good, good. I'm fine now.* In the next three hours I cleaned the entire house. All of it. Including areas such as the top of the fridge, the light switch, under the bed, the inside part of the toilet's water tank, everything. *It's September, it's almost New Year's Eve, and I will travel for four weeks in two days. This is just the right time to clean the house.* Come on, girl. You know you're just actively procrastinating...

Have you ever dreaded starting something so much that even cleaning parts of your home that have *never* been cleaned before seemed like a better option? You know what I mean.

After a Marie Kondo-like cleaning, organizing and long bubble bath, I awkwardly sat in front of my little bunny journal. A Noteworthy Thought...

I opened it. Here is my first entry:

I hate this. It makes me feel uncomfortable and awkward. I procrastinated all day just to avoid doing this. Why? Because I have a natural disdain for discomfort. I get annoyed if something uncomfortable gets on my thought radar.

Whoa! What just happened? I never thought about myself like that! An inner voice whispered to me, "*Go on.*"

I won't 'go on' here as this book is not for me. It's for you. I must add that if you are looking for pretty pictures, fancy doodles and advice on how to organize your day better, this book is not for you. This is not a journal. This is a book about how to put your thoughts down in a journal; how to ask meaningful questions and make useful observations about your inner world. And, ultimately, how to make some discoveries that you couldn't have otherwise—and hopefully change your life.

I started this book by saying, "When we live inside our own heads, we can't find better solutions to our problems." This is true when you obsess about your anxieties or obliviously live with a lot of judgment, prejudice, anger and shame. But once you put these thoughts down on paper (and optionally talk to a licensed therapist about them) they are out in the world. They are not in your head anymore. They get a body, a shape, even a voice if you care to read your journal entries out loud.

- What do you think about them now?
- Do they still make sense?
- Are they really that sound?
- Do you really think that about yourself?
- Can you prove that you are like that?
- Are your actions in accordance with your beliefs?

- Who are you? Truly?
- What do you want in life?

These questions may sound average, unimportant or not deep enough. But do you truly know the answer to them? The down-to-earth, honest-to-God, fact-checked answer?

Well, I didn't. To some of them I still don't. If by admitting this I lose all credibility as a self-help author, please, put down the book, return it. I understand your decision. Maybe I would do the same. Maybe there is a person out there who claims that they have it all figured out. Good for them—but I want to stop being one of them.

There was a time when I *felt* like I knew it all. I lived a self-sustaining life through much of my teenage years to my mid-twenties as I came from a poor family. I have a mom whose personality was stolen when I was seven by an insidious illness, schizophrenia. I was trapped in a toxic and abusive relationship in my late teenage years all the way to my early twenties. I dealt with that stuff. I survived them. I didn't become a serial killer, a bank robber or anything similar in the process. I must have something right. *Right?*

Wrong. The only thing I figured out was how to not die—in spirit and body. I learned how to lead a tolerable-to-good life by developing good routines and by becoming flexible and adaptable. I shared my insights about these things in my previous books.

But I never understood how my early traumas affected my day-to-day life in the present. Worse, I didn't know that I didn't know. I was self-assured about me knowing better to a harmful extent. And anyone in my close circle who dared question my 'maturity'—oh boy, I spit hellfire. *I have worked since I was 14. I carried car tires, I washed bloody meat containers and I worked two jobs with three shifts* —and *did my Master's degree. How dare you question my maturity?*

A very immature and tunnel vision-y thing to say in retrospect.

I discovered not long ago that my past traumas did leave scars in my psyche, and my untreated scars were wounding people around me. I didn't know this; and when people tried to tell me, I stayed blind and deaf out of fear. All of my personality, all of my three-decades reality was at stake after all. If my behavior was wrong and I didn't change my beliefs during that time, it meant that I was in the wrong all my life. That's scary shit to digest. So scary, in fact, that some people run away from it all their lives. Thanks to my readings, my therapist and my journaling work, I found out that I was more emotionally immature, selfish, irresponsible, avoidant, mean and empathy-lacking than I ever imagined. After this realization I also knew instantly that I didn't want to be that person anymore. I didn't know these things about myself before, but now I did and I wanted to change them. And so my journey of self-discovery-slash-change began...

Now, after all the reasons I listed about why I'm not qualified to write this book, let me tell you why I am.

Because I'm capable of getting to know myself and then change what I dislike. And more importantly, I believe this with all my heart. Even more importantly, I believe that you are capable of doing this, too. You and me, we all share common things in life; we share similar fears, misconceptions, hopes, struggles, questions and joyful moments. We can help each other. We can lift each other up. My mistakes can turn out to be helpful guidance for you. My story could make you feel less alone, more heard or understood. I would feel very happy if this happened.

Or it might not resonate with you at all. I'm not writing the gospel here, after all. If that's the case, I'm sorry. I wanted to help you so much. But hey, this is something we need to learn to accept, too; that not everyone will agree with us and we won't agree with everybody. And that's fine. If you are looking for directions in life, there are many other books out there that may have been written just for you. I hope you'll find it.

Ultimately, I'm qualified to write this book because the journaling process I describe here helped me. A lot. I won't lie—I'm early in this journey. But as a friend and role model of mine, Derek Sivers, said, "Teach whatever you've learned immediately after learning it while you still remember what it's like to not know it. Once you get used to knowing it, you can't imagine what it's like to not know." The journey to 'discover who you are' is a lifelong one. It's never too early or too late to start this journey. Just because you spent only a few months on this road so far doesn't mean that you can't help.

I'm in a phase of transition now. From 'I don't know

that I don't know', I stepped into the realm of 'I know that I don't know'. So I'm working hard to figure that mythical 'it' out. What is this 'it'? Myself.

- What do I like and what am I like? Why?
- How am I in reality versus how I wish to be? Why?
- What are the things I can really excel at? Why?
- What are the things among these that I truly love or hate doing? Why?
- What are my true, core, I-act-on-them-every-day values and beliefs? Why?
- Which of these are unhealthy, hurtful or in the need of urgent evaluation? Why?
- Who do I want to be today? Tomorrow? In a year? Why?
- What else could or should I ask that is important yet I failed to think about so far?

Have you ever wondered about these questions? (Why?)

If so, come, join me in this journaling journey and let's find the answers together.

Before You Get Started

This book is about the journaling practices you can use to better understand:

- your thoughts and emotions;
- why they reoccur in your life in a predictable manner;
- why you sometimes self-sabotage;
- why and how your actions can hurt people around you;
- why you adopted your bad behavioral and cognitive habits and how you can overwrite them;
- what awaits you on a personal-transformation journey; and

- ultimately who your true self is—restless to present itself

I structured what I have to say into four chapters. Each chapter talks about a crucial step in self-discovery/change. These step are built upon each other. Do your journaling work conscientiously chapter by chapter. Don't skip anything even if you think, *oh, I know this already*. You know it? Great, in that case it will take you less time to complete the exercise. But collect every relevant thought about my questions in one place: a journal.

Here, I'd like to ask you to stop reading for a moment. Before you go on, you'll need a very important accessory to this book. Yes, my friend, you guessed it right. A journal. I created a journal tailor-made for this book. You can download it for free clicking here: zoemckey.com/media/complimentary-journal.docx. This journal is tailor made to this book. As you read the contents of the book, you'll be able to use my physical (printable) journal to fill in with your thoughts.

If you are not interested in the physical journal I made to accompany this book, it's fine. You can get any fillable journal from any store and just write down the questions yourself as indicated in this book. You can also use a simple Word document and record your thoughts digitally. I'm an old-fashioned Pinterest junkie. I like pretty physical journals but hey, this is your journal and it has to fit your needs.

Okay, I think I gave you all the necessary need-to-knows. Let's dig in to our mind!

1

Step One: Awareness

In this chapter we will talk about how aware we are about our emotions and our behavior in general. Do we behave maturely in our interactions with others or are we being unreasonable and immature without realizing? How does our behavior affect our relationships and our view of ourselves? The goal of this chapter is to gain necessary awareness of our habitual behavior patterns and emotional (im)maturity level.

LET me list some behaviors and then you can tell me if you recognize yourself in any of them.

- I often overreact to relatively small problems;
- I don't express a lot of empathy or emotional awareness;
- I feel uncomfortable when it comes to emotional closeness;
- I'm often irritated by others' different points of view or differences;
- I sometimes use people as confidants but I don't feel I am a good listener in return;
- I feel I'm often inconsistent with my reactions. Sometimes I can react harshly, sometimes calmly to the same situation;
- If someone requires my advice on an emotional problem, I either give a superficial answer or become bothered. I cannot truly empathize;
- Even minor disagreements or criticism can make me very defensive;
- I often argue based on what I feel, not based on facts and logic;
- People tell me I'm seldom self-reflective / I have a victim attitude / I don't look for my role in a problem; and
- I feel discomfort when I'm asked to be more

open-minded, receptive to new ideas or experiences[1]

HOW MANY OF these sentences describe your behavior? According to psychologist and bestselling author, Lindsay C. Gibson, these are signs of potential emotional immaturity. She highlights that to consider any of the statements relevant in your case, they must happen repeatedly as a behavior pattern to be considered a real warning sign of emotional immaturity. These patterns show up so automatically and unconsciously that you are often unaware of them. If you really want to get to the bottom of the question "*Does this statement apply to me?*" ask three close friends or relatives to share their observations about you in light of the given statements.

OCCASIONAL EMOTIONAL REGRESSIONS can happen to anyone; even Buddhist priests snap from time to time, or become impulsive after a tiring or stressful day.

. . .

EMOTIONALLY IMMATURE PEOPLE are seldom self-reflective; they don't think about how their behavior affects others either. They are not very familiar or comfortable with apologizing or expressing regret.

WHY AM I insisting on talking about emotional immaturity? Based on my research and personal experience, it can be a huge roadblock between our current selves and our best selves. Don't worry, I'm not here to judge you. I am one of the greatest (recovering, but still) emotionally immature people I know! Anything I say in this book applies to me, too. If you recognize yourself, don't be ashamed—we share the burden, my friend.

I'M ABSOLUTELY guilty of many of the statements mentioned above. Thanks to reading *Adult Children of Emotionally Immature Parents* by Lindsay C. Gibson and my journaling activity I discovered from where some of these patterns are coming from and how profoundly they affect my life.

. . .

HERE IS WHAT I DID: I wrote down in my journal on a blank page each sentence that I felt was more true than not in my case. For example:

"EVEN MINOR DISAGREEMENTS or criticism can make me very defensive."

THAT'S JUST SO ME. No wonder it was one of the first issues I started analyzing. When you face a similar *aha* moment about yourself, the best first question you can ask yourself is, "*Why?*"

"WHY DO minor disagreements or criticism trigger me and make me defensive?"

THEN ANSWER YOUR QUESTION HONESTLY. Here is what I figured out:

"BECAUSE I FEEL that if people don't agree with me, they will have a lower opinion of me. They won't like me, they won't consider me 'one of them' or like-

minded so they will leave me for someone else who shares their opinion. When I was younger my subconscious go-to response to this was changing my opinion and agreeing with people no matter what. Later in life I became super defensive about my stances and tried to convince others about my point of view no matter what."

THERE, the ugly truth. It's not an earth-shattering revelation—somewhere deep down I knew I acted this way. But these observations never got to the level of conscious understanding and thus never got to the point of them being a recognized issue. Thus they didn't get resolved; they just festered and festered, making me more and more anxious and bitter. This oozing negativity and repression affected people around me. Sometimes, after either people pleasing or having a harsh argument due to my defensiveness, I would just sit and contemplate:

"WHY DID I DO THAT? What was the point of defending or ditching my opinion? How did either of these actions make my life better? I don't feel happier.

What motivates me every time to enter this wicked spiral of impulsive actions?"

I'M sure that many of us have been in this state of mind; we can't understand why we act a certain way or why we say things we know by experience won't bring us the results we want, but we go along with them anyway. The problem is that many of us consider impulsive or people-pleasing behavior as an unchangeable aspect of ourselves, not only a learned, habitual reaction to an emotional cue. *This is me. That's who I am,* we may think. But is that really the case?

ACCORDING TO MY OWN EXPERIENCES, this is a false belief. Sure, genetics and temperament play some role in how irritable or confrontation-averse we are. But only to a certain extent. When it comes to reactions, we can always choose to do better.

CHARLES DUHIGG, the author of the book *The Power of Habit,* states that habits work in a loop system. There is always a cue that triggers the habit, the habitual response to that cue and a reward for which we perform the habitual response. Let's interpret Mr. Duhigg's habit loop in the case of my example.

- **The Cue:** Some kind of disagreement.
- **The Reward:** Feeling safe, accepted and worthy. (At the end of the day this is what my people pleasing and defensiveness boils down to.)
- **The Habitual Response:** Either changing my mind about my opinion to please, or trying to make others change their opinion to match mine.[2]

NEEDLESS TO SAY, both of those responses are wrong. If I change my mind about my opinion to please, I'm dishonest; both to myself and to others. People can sense dishonesty and they won't trust me after a while as they will know I won't give them real feedback. If I defend my opinion at all costs, I come across as stubborn, selfish, egoistical or even narcissistic. People will feel uncomfortable talking to me and while they might end up agreeing with me for the sake of peace, they will feel resentment towards me and avoid me in the future.

I FIGURED all this out thanks to my journaling. Again, I know it is not rocket science but I hardly ever thought about my actions in this analytical way before. I was recycling memories without intention or direction; just raging and raging without ever seeking a way out of that cycle. Putting my thoughts down on paper and asking meaningful questions about them helped me gain clarity on who I truly was. And yes, I discovered that there were some aspects about my behavior that I didn't like.

I ADMITTED to myself that I wanted to have a calm life with no anger and bitterness—I just never had that life before so it was easier to pretend that it didn't exist. It was much more familiar to just rage even if it hurt because at least I knew how to do it. I didn't know how to not rage when I felt anger. When my boyfriend told me that he is often angry too but he can release this anger without an explosion, I was puzzled. *Is that possible?* My father, my mother, everyone in my close circle deals with anger the explosive way. It didn't even occur to me that things could go differently as I didn't know any better. That was my reality.

WHEN MY BOYFRIEND told me that one fight a month is a lot I was shocked. *I had a fight a day in my previous relationships, dude, you should feel lucky*, I thought. "I don't think that once a month is a lot," I said.

I FELT EXTREMELY defensive about my shit. Back in the day, I interpreted his remark of having too many conflicts as him being the jerk for not accepting my reality; you know, the reality where smashing plates and cursing is just a regular Saturday activity. I felt entitled and enraged because of him not being more compromising, to meet in the middle: *how about one fight every two weeks?*

HERE COMES THE MIND-BLOWING TWIST: I hated fighting. I hate fighting. I detest that adrenaline rush, the lack of control, the exhaustion I feel after a confrontation so much... Yet, I still defended this hated state because it was familiar. It was easier to defend it, to do it and keep hating it than to admit that I was in the wrong, I was the one with the worse behavioral habit, the one who should have strived for the more constructive, loving and peaceful conflict resolution pattern he knew. It's insane; and yet one can live with this insanity for decades without ever questioning it.

WE CAN ASK questions in this struggle like, "Why does this happen to me? Why do I deserve this?" Wrong questions, sister. "Why do I do this to myself?" is a much more legit way to approach the subject. But to be able to ask this question, one needs a certain amount of self-awareness. That's the hard part; to get the awareness and then the courage to own our mistakes.

WHEN, thanks to Lindsay C. Gibson's book, I gained my minimal awareness, I wanted to know if I was really that immature. I knew I could be biased, so to gain absolute clarity on my new discoveries, I asked some of my closest friends what they thought regarding my conflict handling habits. They confirmed my fears. Some of the responses were not pretty.

"DO you know how much I had to swallow because you were not listening to me and were so defensive all the time? I felt like I was walking on eggshells around you. I never knew when you'd disagree and, as a consequence, how badly you'd react. I felt very unhappy."

"YES, I knew you had this tendency. That's why I never brought up certain topics. I knew you couldn't handle them."

"YES, I tried to tell you this a few times but you became very defensive. So..."

ARE you familiar with the feeling of profound shame? The kind of shame that lights your cheeks on fire and then it spreads downward in your body making your stomach tingle uncomfortably, making your limbs numb and settling deep in your belly like a heavy rock? Your mind goes blank and all you can think of is, *Please, Earth, just swallow me right now, I don't want to feel this?* Well, that's how I felt. I must repeat they were not random people from the streets. They were my closest friends. People were tiptoeing around me for years and I never realized. I simply did not realize. I wasn't aware—I didn't understand.

AFTER I WENT through the first shockwaves I knew that I couldn't live my life from that moment onward the way I lived it in the past. I just couldn't. I wasn't aware of hurting so many people, but my lack of awareness didn't make their hurt any less painful.

IF YOU GET to a point of such a mental breakdown or spiritual awakening[3] (as Brene Brown defines self-discovery moments as this) there are two things you should do and one thing you shouldn't.

LET'S START with the one you shouldn't do: Don't hate yourself. Don't say bad things to yourself such as, "You are a blind idiot, a hurtful monster, a plague on humanity, all you do is take and damage..." Okay, I don't want to give you ideas. That's not the right behavior for multiple reasons but mostly because it won't bring you to the solution for the problem.

CONTRARY TO WHAT WE THINK, people who truly care about us don't want us to belittle and crush ourselves after we realize we wronged them in some way. They want us to:

- own our actions with a straight back;
- take responsibility;
- admit the wrongdoing;
- express honest regret;
- say sorry; and
- eventually, when they are ready to forgive us, to do everything possible to make up for our mistakes

AND OF COURSE, not repeat a behavior that we

identified as hurtful and harmful in the future. This takes us to the two things that we should do.

1. First and foremost, find a way to change the hurtful and harmful behavior. Charles Duhigg says that our focus should fall on changing the habitual response in the loop, not the cue or the reward. In other words, we need to change the reaction we give to a certain trigger in order to get the reward which we are craving. Craving is another important factor in forming or maintaining a habit. We crave the reward once we face the cue so we perform our habit to get the reward. This sort of craving is dangerous because it elicits an automatized—often bad —response that can bring us trouble.

IN MY CASE the cue was disagreement and discomfort. The reward was feeling safe, accepted and worthy. The wrong habitual response was snapping or pleasing. And the most ironic fact is that due to this habitual response, I never actually got the reward I was craving. All I had achieved was a short-term steam release which was followed either by a strong sense of inferiority in the case of people pleasing or by a strong sense of guilt if I snapped at my loved ones or even strangers. That's when I started understanding that my real perceived reward was not only the feeling of safety, acceptance and worthiness but also the release of steam. (You see, there are so many layers to the onion of self-understanding.)

HOW CAN I change my habitual reaction to get my desired rewards? This is it. This is the question where true change resides. This is the point where you can involve a therapist and brainstorm together for solutions. What I came up with Andrea was this:

- **Notice the cue.** Notice how you become irritated and recognize the familiar feeling, then recall what happens next. You know through experience that your habitual response won't take you to the desired reward. Even if you feel that your defense is righteous, or your pleasing is an easier choice, resist doing either of them.

- **Depersonalize the disagreement.** Disagreements are not about you. No one tries to attack you with them, and by simply having different opinions on things you won't lose anyone. (If you act out and snap, it's a different story.) Every person has their own mind, experiences and opinions, which sometimes are different than your own. It's totally natural and normal. Their opinion is neither more nor less important than yours. Trying to diminish or magnify it is not a healthy thing to do.

- Instead of falling into either-or thinking, **try to understand the other person's side by listening to what they have to say**. In exchange, tell them your side. Be ready that they will accept that you think as you think but they may not agree with you—or vice versa. That's normal. Who told you that you have to agree with everyone or you'll die alone?

THIS LAST QUESTION takes us to point two of the two things we should do after getting to an emotional breakdown or spiritual awakening.

1. **Where is the harmful pattern coming from?**

EVER SINCE I started thinking somewhat critically about myself, I thought that the most important aspect of change was understanding where some bad patterns come from. As I learned more about my past I realized that just because I understood where my bad habits came from, life itself wouldn't be better. Unless I change my behavior consciously and committedly, everything will stay the same. Only this time, it will be worse because I'm conscious about making a mistake yet I do it anyway. This is why discovering our past is only the second step in my current curriculum. It is an important step but not a life-changing one. That's step one described above.

UNDERSTANDING where some of our patterns come from is crucial for emotional healing, self-forgiveness and the forgiveness of others. Some of us (hands up here) can start believing that they are fundamentally flawed people by nature. With such a negative view of ourselves, we can easily mistake habits for personality and learned behavior as temperament coded in our genes. Without realizing that most of our bad habits root in learned patterns during childhood we can easily get stuck in a defeatist attitude where we don't even try to change because 'that's how I am and I can't change that'.

CHILDHOOD EMOTIONAL TRAUMA therapist Andrea Brant, Ph.D. says that as children, we want to please our parents because we crave their love. This craving pushes us to adopt behaviors and opinions that we think will make them accept and love us more. Can you see how early we engage in the cue/habit/reward loop due to our cravings? The more we enforce our neural pathways with such practices the stronger this false self we are creating will become. "When we bury our emotions, we lose touch with who we really are, because our feelings are an integral part of us. We live our lives terrified that if we let the mask drop, we'll no longer be cared for, loved, or accepted," Brant says.[4]

OUR THOUGHTS and beliefs about who we are can empower or disempower us. If we usually berate ourselves in our mind we may end up believing that we don't have control over our lives. We adopt a victim mentality. This is an incorrect way of looking at ourselves. We always have a choice. We can't choose the circumstances we were born in but we can choose to rise above them and live a life in which we feel worthy and lovable.

ALL THIS BEING SAID, the easiest way to accurately assess our childhood baggage is with the help of a therapist. They have studied for many years and are familiar with patterns we wouldn't even think of.

We might think we're just saying something casual like, "My dad always taught me to not allow anyone to step on me—ever." The therapist, on the other hand, can point out to us why this parental wisdom can be dangerous, especially if the father in question acts as if no one else's opinion would be valid compared to his. In our child psyche, our dad's behavior and advice can start a behavior pattern that leads us to not accept others' viewpoints and when they disagree with ours, we feel they 'step on us' so we become defensive.

AND VOILÀ, the loop closes on my story and why I am so defensive. As a kid I wanted to please my father above everything else. I listened to everything he said as if it was the gospel and proudly told him each occasion when I acted as he taught me: "Don't allow anyone to step on you." Then he rewarded me with a 'good job' or an 'I'm proud of you'. Before I knew it, I became this little egocentric defense machine. As a kid, puffing your cheeks and tromping with your feet can seem endearing, but in adulthood defensiveness and the inability to accept opposing opinions become huge disadvantages—especially with people who have healthy boundaries.

. . .

CHANCES ARE, if you can identify with my shortcomings presented in this chapter, or any other signs-of-emotional-immaturity statement from the beginning of this chapter, you may hurt some people with your bad behavioral habits. While you may not be at fault for how you were educated as a child, when you couldn't understand that these emotionally immature parts of you were harmful, from now on it is your responsibility to change, improve and make amends to those you hurt.

APOLOGIZING IS NOT ALWAYS EASY. It doesn't come naturally to many of us, especially if we come from a home where apologizing and taking responsibility for bad actions was not habitual. The steps of a good apology include the following:

- Honestly admitting that we realize we were wrong;
- Telling the person how we wronged them;
- Empathizing by telling them how we think

they must have felt by our actions and then asking for confirmation or correction;

- Letting the hurt party express their anguish. We shouldn't interrupt, defend ourselves or get caught up in the details. (For example, it doesn't matter if we hurt them Wednesday or Thursday.);
- Sincerely saying sorry for what we have done. Expressing honest regret;
- Committing ourselves not to make the same mistake again and assuring the hurt party about it;
- Asking the hurt party what else we can do to make them feel better. How can we make restitution? and
- Eventually asking for forgiveness. (Make sure to not rush the hurt party into forgiving you. Let them have their own phase of processing their pain.)

PRO TIP to those who can't or don't know how to apologize properly: I read two great books on the topic. One, my personal favorite, is *The Book of Forgiveness* by Desmond Tutu. Mr. Tutu is a South-

African archbishop but I promise you that the book is a great fit for both religious and non-religious readers. He uses some examples of Jesus Christ and stories from the Bible but they are very relatable and he doesn't try to shovel them down anyone's throat. This book will help you understand the steps of a proper apology when you seek forgiveness, how to develop the capacity to honestly forgive, and last but not least, how to forgive yourself. The book has fascinating, heart-breaking, terrifying stories, and real miracles. It's also a very educational book as it presents life in South Africa during and after the apartheid regime. I think everybody should learn about it—and this book gives a valuable glimpse.[5]

THE OTHER BOOK is *When Sorry Isn't Enough* by Gary Chapman and Jennifer Thomas. This book is a great complimentary piece to the Desmond Tutu book as it explains why and how some type of apologies (apology languages) are a better fit with someone than other types. If you are familiar with Chapman's groundbreaking work "The Five Love Languages" you can assess what to expect from this book. I hope they will help you.[6]

. . .

THE ANSWER to the question "Why do some people never discover themselves?" lies in the chapter itself. The process of self-discovery I described is a tough one. Admitting as adults that we are emotionally immature, selfish, entitled or wrong —especially if we indeed are all of these things—is almost an impossible mission. Because by admitting these things we also have to face the ugly reality that the life we've lived so far was flawed; that we hurt people, deceived ourselves, didn't live up to our true potential. Some people are unable to make this step. Even if they feel it deep down that the characteristics of emotional immaturity apply to them and hurt them greatly, they will brush it off, throw the book away, give me a one-star review and live on. I don't blame them.

I LIVED for three decades an unhealthy, false identity packed with habits I adopted to please another unhealthy, false identity—my father. It is very difficult to type these words, you know. He was my hero, my best friend—or so I thought. I love him and I know that he is a good person at his core but he allowed a lot of his bad habits to fester in him and in others around him. He is a smart person who reads a lot of books. I'm sure he came across this topic during his lifetime, yet he failed to internalize the information and change.

THERE ARE many people like my dad out there; who fight and fight the currents of life, get overwhelmed, collapse and wonder why the world is against them. Then they get up and fight even harder because in their mind they failed because of not fighting fiercely enough. It doesn't occur to them that the fighting itself is the issue. There is no fight out there. Your life won't get better if you win a fight with someone else. Only if you win a fight against yourself: your bad habits. As the number of your bad habits decreases and you approach your true self, your inner fights will cease as well. You'll be at peace.

Journal Mode

Don't worry; I won't skip the 'how-to-journal' part. At the end of each chapter I will give a brief summary on how to apply the information shared in the chapter to your own problems, in your own journal, at home.

This chapter talked about how to discover our emotionally immature behaviors and how to dig deeper to understand where they are coming from; when, how and why they manifest; and how to change these aspects of our behavior.

Here are the steps that you can use as guidance:

1. Take each bullet point you answered 'true'

to and, one by one, write them down on a separate page in your journal. (To make your job easier, I will insert the bullet points below.)

- I often overreact to relatively small problems;
- I don't express a lot of empathy or emotional awareness;
- I feel uncomfortable when it comes to emotional closeness;
- I'm often irritated by others' different points of view or differences;
- I sometimes use people as confidants but I don't feel I am a good listener in return;
- I feel I'm often inconsistent with my reactions. Sometimes I can react harshly, sometimes calmly to the same situation;
- If someone requires my advice on an emotional problem I either give a superficial answer or become bothered. I cannot truly empathize;
- Even minor disagreements or criticism can make me very defensive;
- I often argue based on what I feel, not based on facts and logic;

- People tell me I'm seldom self-reflective / I have a victim attitude / I don't look for my role in a problem; and
- I feel discomfort when I'm asked to be more open-minded and receptive to new ideas or experiences

1. Use the *five whys* technique on each bullet point. For example: I often overreact relatively small problems. *Why?* [Your answer.] *Why?* [Your answer.] *Why?* So on and so forth. Give yourself time to reflect on each *why* layer. Don't rush, you're not in a hurry. Recall specific events that prove that the bullet point indeed applies to you.[1]

1. Note down a few of these specific events and try to identify the common pattern in them. What is your cue? What is the habitual reaction to that cue? What reward are you seeking? What's the craving that triggers this habit loop in you? Write them down for at least four to five different events. Look for commonalities.

1. By keeping the cue and reward, come up

with at least three alternative reactions you could give to the emotionally immature habit in question. These alternatives should be responsible, harmless, adult reactions. (I will discuss what emotional maturity is in a later chapter.)

1. Try to identify what the origin of this emotional immature habit is. Try to recall a person from your past who has the same reactions or had the same beliefs. There is a strong possibility that it will be one of your parents, grandparents or another close adult figure from your childhood. Write down what this person did—how did they contribute to your current behavior? What was your motivation in adopting this habit? To please this person, to try to be different than this person (yes, it can happen often that we try to be different on purpose and end up becoming the same without noticing it)?

1. Make a list of people your bad habit has affected in a negative way. If you wish to truly ease your soul, apologize to them. If

the person you hurt is not alive anymore or is out of reach, do the good old write-a-letter-then-burn-it exercise. I would recommend not burning it but just tearing it apart—it's safer.

Pro tip: use a colorful post-it if you run out of space. For example, you thought you finished point 1 and started writing point 2, but something else came up in your mind. Don't let that valuable information get away. Write it on a post-it and stick it above point 1. Keep information together and with every detail.

Complimentary Journal for Chapter 1:

a.) This is the list of emotionally immature behaviors from Chapter 1. If you recognize yourself in any of them put an X next to those that apply to you.

- I often overreact to relatively small problems; ___
- I don't express a lot of empathy or emotional awareness; ___
- I feel uncomfortable when it comes to emotional closeness; ___
- I'm often irritated by others' different points of view or differences; ___
- I sometimes use people as confidants but I don't feel I am a good listener in return; ___
- I feel I'm often inconsistent with my

reactions. Sometimes I can react harshly, sometimes calmly to the same situation; ___

- If someone requires my advice on an emotional problem, I either give a superficial answer or become bothered. I cannot truly empathize; ___
- Even minor disagreements or criticism can make me very defensive; ___
- I often argue based on what I feel, not based on facts and logic; ___
- People tell me I'm seldom self-reflective / I have a victim attitude / I don't look for my role in a problem; ___
- I feel discomfort when I'm asked to be more open-minded, receptive to new ideas or experiences[1] ___
- Add more emotionally immature behaviors that you can think of yourself doing:
- ______________________________
- ______________________________
- ______________________________

b.) Write each of the emotionally immature behaviors you identified with to the exercise panel below – one at the time – and analyze them with the help of the five whys technique:

(I prepared the exercise panel for five behaviors. If you identified with less than five statements, leave the unnecessary sections blank. If you identified with more than five statements, just grab an empty sheet of paper, design it the same way I did and continue with Behavior #6, Behavior #7 etc. If you need guidance on how to complete this exercise, use Chapter 1's Journal Mode section.)

Behavior #1:

Why?

Why?

Why?

____

____

____

Why?

____

____

____

Why?

____

____

____

Behavior #2:

____

Why?

____

____

____

Why?

____

____

____

Why?

____

____

____

Why?

____

____

____

Why?

____

Behavior #3:

Why?

Why?

Why?

Why?

____

____

____

Why?

____

____

____

Behavior #4:

____

Why?

____

____

____

Why?

____

____

____

Why?

____

____

____

Why?

____

____

____

Why?

____

____

____

Behavior #5:

____

Why?

____

____

____

Why?

____

____

____

Why?

____

____

____

Why?

____

____

____

Why?

____

____

____

c.) Time to find a way to change the hurtful and harmful behaviors you identified and explored in points a.) and b.). These behaviors are bad habits thus they can be changed.

Take the same behaviors, write them down again, but now answer the following questions about them:

Behavior #1:

____

What's the cue that triggers this behavior?

____

____

____

What's the regular reaction I give to this cue?

____

____

____

What outcome (reward) am I seeking?

____

____

____

What is the other person feeling when I perform this bad habit? What is he/she trying to say? (Put yourself in the other person's shoes.)

____

____

____

How can I depersonalize this disagreement I have?

____

____

____

Alternative reactions I can give as a response to the triggering cue to fulfill the following self-requirements: acting in accordance with the type of person I'd like to be; acting in a way that doesn't hurt the other person; acting in a way to get the reward I'm seeking without 'side effects':

1.

____

____

____

2.

____

____

____

3.

____

____

____

Behavior #2:

____

What's the cue that triggers this behavior?

____

____

____

What's the regular reaction I give to this cue?

____

____

____

What outcome (reward) am I seeking?

____

____

____

What is the other person feeling when I perform this bad habit? What is he/she trying to say? (Put yourself in the other person's shoes.)

____

____

____

How can I depersonalize this disagreement I have?

____

____

____

Alternative reactions I can give as a response to the triggering cue to fulfill the following self-requirements: acting in accordance with the type of person I'd like to be; acting in a way that doesn't hurt the other person; acting in a way to get the reward I'm seeking without 'side effects':

1.

____

____

____

2.

____

____

____

3.

____

____

____

Behavior #3:

____

What's the cue that triggers this behavior?

____

____

____

What's the regular reaction I give to this cue?

____

____

____

What outcome (reward) am I seeking?

____

____

____

What is the other person feeling when I perform this bad habit? What is he/she trying to say? (Put yourself in the other person's shoes.)

____

____

____

How can I depersonalize this disagreement I have?

____

____

____

Alternative reactions I can give as a response to the triggering cue to fulfill the following self-requirements: acting in accordance with the type of person I'd like to be; acting in a way that doesn't hurt the other person; acting in a way to get the reward I'm seeking without 'side effects':

1.

____

____

____

2.

____

____

____

3.

____

____

____

Behavior #4:

____

What's the cue that triggers this behavior?

____

____

____

What's the regular reaction I give to this cue?

____

____

____

What outcome (reward) am I seeking?

____

____

____

What is the other person feeling when I perform this bad habit? What is he/she trying to say? (Put yourself in the other person's shoes.)

____

____

____

How can I depersonalize this disagreement I have?

____

____

____

Alternative reactions I can give as a response to the triggering cue to fulfill the following self-requirements: acting in accordance with the type of person I'd like to be; acting in a way that doesn't hurt the other person; acting in a way to get the reward I'm seeking without 'side effects':

1.

____

____

____

2.

____

____

____

3.

____

____

____

Behavior #5:

____

What's the cue that triggers this behavior?

____

____

____

What's the regular reaction I give to this cue?

____

____

____

What outcome (reward) am I seeking?

____

____

____

What is the other person feeling when I perform this bad habit? What is he/she trying to say? (Put yourself in the other person's shoes.)

____

____

____

How can I depersonalize this disagreement I have?

____

____

____

Alternative reactions I can give as a response to the triggering cue to fulfill the following self-requirements: acting in accordance with the type of person I'd like to be; acting in a way that doesn't hurt the other person; acting in a way to get the reward I'm seeking without 'side effects':

1.

____

____

____

2.

____

____

____

3.

____

____

____

d.) Look for commonalities in the behaviors you just analyzed in points b.) and c.). Can you recognize any repeating patterns? Do some of these behaviors stem from the same negative emotion? (anger, impatience, lack of empathy, fear, loneliness, hurt etc.) Identify as many common aspects of the different behaviors as possible:

____

____

____

____

____

____

____

____

____

____

____

____

____

____

____

e.) Identify what's the origin of the emotional immature behaviors. Who is the person from your past, who had the same reactions, or beliefs? Write down what did this person do, how did he or she contribute to your current behavior? What was your motivation in adopting this habit? (Pleasing this person, trying to be different than this person etc.)

Behavior #1:

____

The person I learned this behavior from:

____

How did he/she contribute to my current behavior?

____

____

____

Why did I adopt his/her behavior?

____

____

____

Behavior #2:

____

The person I learned this behavior from:

____

How did he/she contribute to my current behavior?

____

____

____

Why did I adopt his/her behavior?

____

____

____

Behavior #3:

____

The person I learned this behavior from:

____

How did he/she contribute to my current behavior?

____

____

____

Why did I adopt his/her behavior?

____

____

____

Behavior #4:

____

The person I learned this behavior from:

____

How did he/she contribute to my current behavior?

____

____

____

Why did I adopt his/her behavior?

____

____

____

Behavior #5:

____

The person I learned this behavior from:

____

How did he/she contribute to my current behavior?

____

____

____

Why did I adopt his/her behavior?

____

____

____

f.) Make a list of people your bad habit has affected in a negative way. If you wish to truly ease your soul, apologize to them. If the person you hurt is not alive anymore or is out of reach, do the good old write-a-letter-then-burn-it exercise. I would recommend not burning it but just tearing it apart—it's safer.

The list of the people I know I hurt and wish to apologize to:

____

____

____

____

Complimentary Journal for Chapter 1:

2

Step Two: Stop the Blame Game

WHY DO WE BLAME OTHERS FOR OUR MISTAKES? Why are we so mean to ourselves when we make an unwise decision? Emotional immaturity is one major cause behind these two tendencies we often perform. The lack of maturity and self-understanding can also lead us to the false notion that after a hard period in our lives (after a break up, a big fight, getting fired, etc.) we finally learned our lessons and know what to do differently in the future. Unfortunately these 'lessons' that stem in our emotionally immature understanding are flawed; we may conclude that the lesson is we should have been harder and more unforgiving with ourselves, or with others.

Have you ever felt like you've finally got it all figured

out, and from now on everything will be okay? And then something happens and you bounce back with the stern realization that you know less than you thought you knew? That things really don't stay the same forever? We may start blaming others for things not panning out, or we might start telling ourselves hateful things as a means of punishment for daring to hope.

I know, believing that things won't ever change for the better is an extremely childish way of thinking. But put your hand on your heart and tell yourself you never ever have that tingling feeling (or hope) after a period of good events that things now make sense and will stay this good. Isn't it adding an extra boost to your general state of wellbeing to fantasize about the bliss becoming permanent? Maybe you don't. But I'm sure many people do.

Then reality strikes; something bad happens and your life gets back to normal. You suddenly realize that your wishful thinking was incorrect. My reaction to this realization was seldom a healthy one. A good reaction has to do with accepting life's impermanence; give in to the unchangeable reality of human existence, be okay with everything changing and every negative event being an opportunity for growth, seize this change and grow. No, sir. My go-to reaction was this: *I'm stupid to think that I can lead a good life. I never could and never will. Believing that I got it figured out is just another delusion of my stupid mind.* While the last sentence isn't necessarily incorrect, the way I usually phrased it to myself was more than cruel. Can you relate with this problem?

It is a serious self-deception to tell ourselves that we figured everything out already. We start to believe it —and persist believing it even when life proves us otherwise. We won't seek growth in the areas we think are 'settled'. Thus when something goes wrong in these areas we can easily fall into the trap of telling ourselves, "Life is unfair, people are malicious, everybody is against me, nobody gets me, it must be someone else's fault things turned out this way." Can you notice that this attitude shifts responsibility from us to others? It is a dishonest, childish and counterproductive way to handle others and ourselves. There is no room for improvement in shifting blame and self-chosen obliviousness, nor a promise for a better life.

Why is shifting the blame dangerous? Because it's comfortable and seems like a reasonable explanation for our pain. It's much less painful to assume that everybody else is at fault and we are their victims. Doing this gives us much less trouble; we free ourselves mentally from the burden and pain of owning up to our mistakes. We don't feel the need to try to find our contribution in the conflict.

When we start building up this shifting-blame habit we still feel, somewhere deep down, that we are also at fault in a conflict. But the more we repeat the habit, the more we'll start believing it. At some point in life we won't even think about how we should respond to a disagreement, criticism or a conflict of opinion. Rejection, defensiveness, feeling offended and blame will become our automatic go-to plan. How will people react to our behavior? Depends on the person, of course, but no one will feel good about not being heard, or being attacked and blamed.

I'm not saying that you are not right in some cases. Sometimes people indeed are malicious and you should protect your boundaries. But it matters how you do that. As a soldier, there is a difference between shooting every possible moving thing and focusing on the enemy—preparing, aiming and only shooting those who would otherwise shoot us. The first approach might kill us some enemies but will also kill innocent people; people who didn't mean to harm us, people we love, people who fight on our side.

In other words, being mindlessly defensive and blaming the world not only alienates those very few whom we indeed should keep at a distance, but everybody—including people we care about. At the end of the day, we also alienate our true self, our better self. We deprive it of the opportunity to grow, to be better.

You might ask: If you can't ever figure it all out, then what's the point of even trying? I asked myself this question, too. Based on my personal journaling discovery here is what I concluded:

"We don't know every possible disease that could kill us. Shouldn't we at least vaccinate ourselves against the ones we know? Is it really smart to not vaccinate ourselves against anything then? We can't prepare for every life-threatening hazard when we go out into the wilderness. Shouldn't we at least prepare for as many of them as possible? Is it really a better option to go without the minimal safety precautions?"

Chances are that you would answer these questions like, "Yes, sure, I'd vaccinate myself for the diseases I can. Sure, I'd take all the safety precautions that I can before hiking." Deconstructing our bad behavioral habits and replacing them with something better, something that guarantees our 'happiness survival' for longer, works the same way. Just like when we go for a hike, we can't be prepared for everything—especially when we are beginner hikers. One time we'll learn that we should also put a raincoat into our backpack. The next time we learn that mosquito repellents won't protect us from irritating plants so thin-but-long gear is better in some terrains than shorts and a t-shirt. We also learn to select and apply our lessons at the right time. For example, if you hike at the North Pole, your knowledge about mosquitos and thin-but-long gear is hardly helpful.

The same goes for life lessons. Just because you learn to handle one of your shortcomings it doesn't mean that the same handling technique will help you with another type of shortcoming.

The point in trying to become a better you is to live better than the day before. You'll never have all the answers but, every time you open up to discomfort and pain to harness a new lesson, your life will get easier every time the same issue comes up. You won't be immune against every bacterium but at least you'll be immune to those your body successfully defeated.

I know by experience that all this is easier said than done. We get it. We know that blaming others for our mistakes is a bad thing. We also know that blaming ourselves with negative, hateful self-talk is also harmful. We know, but we can't apply the knowledge in those crucial times we'd need it the most; when things fall apart and we're in the situation. The self-reflection part of this chapter will aim to help you with applying your knowledge in times of crisis.

1. **How to overcome the urge to blame others.**

The first step is always awareness. We can't change doing something that we actually think is not wrong. People told me that I had problems with my temper for years. I didn't accept it. I believed that I was right whenever I had an outburst and they were wrong for pushing my buttons when they told me I was in the wrong. *Can't they see how angry I am? How can they still say things like that? They must be very self-absorbed to think that they are right.* Guess who was the self-absorbed one? When you have such a mindset you won't be acting like an adult responsible for their actions for sure.

In my experience, it's especially hard to accept even the most valid criticism from the subject of your anger. For example, if you are mad and acting out on your husband for something, if he is the one who tries to tell you that you are wrong, what will you do? Explode, like Hades in the Disney movie. To gain that initial awareness about your issues therefore is difficult when your only feedback option is the trigger of your bad habit.

What's to be done? You need to gain awareness from external, preferably independent sources. When I say independent, I mean books, a therapist, someone with whom you don't have an emotional connection; not friends and family. They can be a good source of feedback but the chances that they will sugarcoat things or that you won't take them seriously are quite high.

In my case, I had been hearing for a long time that I'm irritable, snappy and often irrational while I argue, but I never stopped questioning my righteousness until I read a book that resonated with my critiques 100 percent. You know that feeling when it hits you: *They might be right.* If a complete stranger, a psychologist, who doesn't know anything about me can nail down my behavior patterns so accurately and call them emotionally immature and harmful, there must be some truth to it. And then the snowball effect kicked in. I read more and more, googled descriptive keywords, got a therapist, started journaling and finally understood why and how I was wrong. I became self-aware.

Strangely enough, ever since, I don't have that instantaneous 'I'm right so you must be wrong' feeling. Now I know how often I was wrong about my actions; especially about things that affect other people. I can't dictate how my behavior should affect them. I need to try putting myself in their shoes and then listen to their side of the story.

I need to be aware of my snapping, hot-headed tendencies. I have to keep in mind that unfortunately, this is my go-to answer to discomfort. Thus whenever I feel discomfort I have to remind myself of my snapping habits and consciously avoid them.

It is helpful to assess the situation objectively. What's happening? I couldn't print my pictures because the InstaPrint in the mall was broken.

(Really, this is a true story.) I complained about this to my boyfriend who just shrugged it off. "So what? We can go to another mall tomorrow and print them there." He meant well, trying to calm me and offering me an alternative solution. What did I get from his response? He doesn't care about my pictures, he doesn't get how much enthusiasm I felt and how hooked I was on this printing project. Wrong direction, girl. Furthermore, I failed to realize that he was calm and in a good/average mood, unlike me. The shitty thing to do here would be to contaminate his mood with such nonsense as an unfulfilled instant InstaPrint dream.

How did my brain work back then? *I can't blame the printer as that's just a printer, I can't blame myself because, duh, where is my fault in this? Who's left there to blame? The carefree guy dispensing non-empathetic and unrequested advice?* You can be sure that the last option was what I went for. The worst thing you can do, sister, the worst.

These are those small, seemingly harmless and unimportant fights that build up in someone, and one day you wake up to see the guy is gone. Either for good or somewhere else where he isn't blamed for everything, feels safe and his mood doesn't get dragged down.

I would like to emphasize that I'm talking about stupid issues here, like the one I just shared above, not about life-altering shocks such as getting a bad diagnosis, having a death in the family, getting fired, etc. In those cases, tell your partner or the person you're having conflict with that you know you'll drag their mood down. Those shocking events call for empathy. (Sure enough, blaming or being mean to your partner isn't a good thing even in those cases.) But let's face it, most of our relationship fights erupt over superficial stuff that shouldn't even be an argument in the first place. Who is guilty of blaming others for our problems, ladies and gentlemen?

Because these are our problems. The real problem is that we even consider things like picture printing, a queue at the bank, a cheeseburger that doesn't have pickle in it, problems. These are annoyances at best. Something that responsible adults with a healthy sense of importance can brush off in most cases as a "So what? Stuff happens."

The real problem is when we fail to contain our negative emotions and contaminate someone else with them. That's an insidious move; why should someone else, especially a loved one, feel bad just because we feel bad?

I'm not talking about when we share our pain and sorrow with someone to seek comfort and understanding. I mean those occasions when we soothe our negative emotions by making someone feel even more miserable than we do; double credit if we also shift the blame on them.

I said the first step in catching yourself before you practice your bad habits is awareness; you need to know and accept that your habitual response is harmful. The second step is *empathy*.

Empathy is the capability to position yourself in someone else's shoes and see a situation from their perspective. For example, your mother says to imagine yourself being in her place and you reply, "How could I guess your feelings? Only you know how you are feeling. Events might affect you differently than they affect me so my guess could be wrong." While you'd think this is a sound way of approaching the problem, it is a dismissive, non-empathetic answer. It sends the message that you won't even bother positioning yourself in your mother's place as nobody but her knows what she feels. This reply would make your mother feel unheard and not cared about. When someone asks for empathy, they don't really ask for a 100-percent accurate brain scan from your side, they just want to feel like you are willing to put aside your opinion and take the time to try and put yourself in their shoes honestly. Even if your diagnosis is not totally accurate or complete, it will make the other person feel that you care about them, and you'll also be more informed about a viewpoint that's different from yours.

Brene Brown, the author of the book *The Power of Vulnerability*, defines these four steps to show empathy:

1. Perspective Taking, or putting yourself in someone else's shoes;
2. Staying out of judgment and listening;
3. Recognizing emotion in another person that you have maybe felt before; and
4. Communicating that you can recognize that emotion[1]

In other words, empathy is not only about trying to think with someone else's head, it's also about trying to find the same emotions you think the other is feeling in your own heart.

Due to my abandonment issues I often feel needy and interpret even the slightest dismissal as total rejection. This is what happened a few days ago when I woke up feeling needy and tried to cuddle with my boyfriend in the morning. He was trying to sleep more so when I started scooting closer to him, he turned his back to me and crawled away. It wasn't even a conscious act—just something a sleeping person would do when they want to sleep more. However, this small gesture made me feel deeply insecure for a moment. Anybody ever try to cuddle and get the cold flip in return? Y'all know what I'm talking about. For a moment that cold rush ran down from my head into my stomach, bringing up thoughts like, *He doesn't love you, he doesn't care about you, he'll leave you right after he brushes his teeth...* When I became aware of these thoughts I stopped for a moment. *Hey, old friends, pain and panic. I see you're here but today I won't engage. I know what you're trying to do,* I told myself. I noted that my partner was still asleep. I also noted that I dismissed him in a similar or even ruder fashion so many times before when I wanted to sleep. Did I want to leave him?

Heck no. Did I hate him? No. I just wanted to sleep. Period. End of story.

I can't describe to you how relieved I felt after my conclusion. I'm not sure what made me happier, the fact that he didn't actually reject me or that I managed to realize this by myself. That morning was a victory for me. A small one but, after all, long-term, bad habits change thanks to many small victories like this one. As you could see in the story, I didn't do anything crazy complicated. I recognized the pattern in time and analyzed the situation with empathy.

What do you do if you fail step one, awareness, or step two, empathy?

We are only human. Even against our best intentions, sometimes we'll fall back to our old, familiar patterns. As Charles Duhigg says, no habit gets eradicated completely. They just get overwritten with a new, more well-practiced one. Overwriting habits and consolidating the new pattern takes time. We'll fall back to our old patterns when we are not present enough, stressed or otherwise distracted; especially at the beginning of our journey. Don't hate yourself if this happens. I know it is difficult not to be self-loathing and hopeless in these cases, but stay strong.

There is no human on planet Earth who can completely overwrite a decades-old habit on the first try—except maybe smokers, but we're not talking about them, and even they face many obstacles. When I say stay strong, I mean be willing to take the experience fully in. *Yes, I did this and I know it's not a good thing to do. What can I learn from this situation to move on with a lesson at least?* Then think about your experience, what triggered it, what your mood was when it happened and how you could handle the situation differently in the future.

There is, however, one thing you can do when you fall back into your old habits for a moment and hurt someone as a consequence: Take responsibility for it quickly and genuinely apologize. People don't expect you to be perfect. They want you to own your mistakes and show remorse when you mess something up. They want to know that you know what you did was wrong and that you recognize the anguish you might have caused.

Once you gain awareness of your shortcomings, you have no excuse to shy away from taking responsibility for your actions while hoping to still come out as a caring, honest person.

Usually, when we do something bad, our gut instinct is to try to sweep it under the rug. *Maybe if I pretend I didn't realize I did a bad thing, or said something wrong, people won't notice it or won't take it personally, they'll forget about it and I will be off the hook.* We try to cover our mistake; pretend that it never happened. In other words we avoid responsibility. Sometimes we don't even do this to escape responsibility. We simply are so ashamed by our actions that it's hard to put our mistake into words, to give our shame a verbalized body. We feel inadequate when we make mistakes and we think that if we speak about them, others will know how inadequate we are.

I used to be totally guilty of this error in thinking. Today I understand that it is much more shameful not to quickly and readily confess my mistakes. Failing to take responsibility and saying sorry as soon as possible will lead people to think that we don't have a spine and are dishonest. People are not stupid; they know when they receive hostile, hurtful or unnecessary negative treatment. Just because we pretend that we didn't catch it, we won't forget about it; if anything, our pretended obliviousness will make them only more resentful towards us. But who can stay resentful when they receive an honest, heartfelt apology? "I know I hurt you and I'm sorry. I acknowledge your pain and want to make up for it." If someone gets this message, they won't stay angry with us. Not for long, at least, and gradually that initial anger will transform into respect and admiration for our ability to own our mistakes.

People possess an incredible power: the power of forgiveness. Archbishop Desmond Tutu in his book *The Book of Forgiving* tells stories of murderers who have been forgiven by the victim's parents. Rape victims, victims of aggression and victims of racism who found the courage in their hearts to forgive their wrongdoers. Conversely, he tells stories of terrorists, murderers and criminals who atoned for their crimes and today are working together with either their victims or the victim's close relatives to make a better world. The moral is that everybody can forgive if they truly want to and everybody can seek forgiveness if they truly regret their deeds.

Taking responsibility, saying sorry and seeking forgiveness liberates us. These actions free us from remorse, guilt and lack of self-respect. This takes us to the next point I wish to talk about: how to overcome our habit of blaming ourselves in a harmful way.

1. **How do you overcome the habit of hateful self-talk?**

Let's play a game. Think about five things that you dislike about yourself, that you consider a flaw or that you resent.

Don't read further. Seriously.

I know it doesn't take much time to the average self-help-reading Joe to fulfill this task—it takes me like five seconds.

Done? Okay.

Now try to list five things that you consider your strengths; things that make you exceptional, lovable and strong. I know. Now is the moment when you roll your eyes and quickly read further or even put the book down, convinced that I'm just messing with you, pushing down your throat some mainstream self-help junk. *Five strengths... sure, I won't think about that stuff.* Am I correct? Did I anticipate your resistance correctly? Maybe, maybe not, but for sure thinking about listing five positive traits is more burdensome than listing the five negatives. Don't worry. It's normal. You are not alone if you felt this way.

Our mind evolutionarily is biased towards the negative. It focuses on weaknesses rather than strengths. While improving your strengths might aid you in hunting down a buffalo rather than an impala, improving your weaknesses could save your life from a lion. The former helps you meet your more complex, dignified needs on the Maslow pyramid like love and belonging, self-esteem and self-fulfillment, but the latter helps you satisfy the most basic needs of all beings, the physiological ones and the ones of safety. The fewer weaknesses our forefathers had, the lower the chances were that they'd end up being the meal.

We are tuned to observe, analyze and evaluate our negative theories of ourselves. We naturally don't think as much about our strengths. In other words, our brain is trained in recalling a negative self-image at any time. However, it is less capable of recalling our positive view about who we are. Neuroscientist and psychologist Daniel Kahneman also discovered that our brain is, by nature, a lazy organ which tries to find cognitive shortcuts and easy answers and happily replaces difficult questions with easier ones or comes up with witty excuses to avoid the question overall.[2]

Now that we talked about all this, I'd humbly ask your brain to take the fatigue just this once to undergo the grind and toss up your top five strengths. (You thought you'd escape this one, didn't you?) If you really want to send me some wow karma vibes, write them down on a paper. This is an optional part but please, think about what the best of you is.

You may feel like, *Okay, girl, I get it. Stop blabbering so much about this trivial task. I will do it, okay? Just stop insisting.* I hear you, my friend. But I won't stop insisting. This is one of the greatest mistakes I made when I tried to improve myself in the past five-six years. Whenever the part of enlisting my strengths, my hopes and my best attributives came up I was brushing the part off, flipping through the pages, and when I finally got to the part that made me think about my negative traits I felt like I had gotten to a safe place. *Good, good. This is what I want. This is what's easy to think about. This is the essential part, right? After all, I want to improve. Improving means discovering and changing the negative, right?*

Sure. But changing for the better also requires objectivity, self-understanding and self-compassion. How can you have any of these things if all you know about yourself is how badly f–ed up you are? Language, I know, but in times like this, who cares? You need to step out of that negative bubble. You are not your bad behavior and especially not only that behavior. It's not enough to vaguely know that you are better than your top five flaws. You are worthy and you are good. You have so many positive building blocks in you. Get to know them! Embrace them! Acknowledge them!

Feel that you are worthy of change.

Believe that whatever hard work stands before you—because changing the bad and ugly, my friend, is hella difficult—is not a waste of effort because it is for someone who is worthy of it. Without having this sense of worthiness, no change will take root. The precondition of worthiness are the positive traits that make your heart fill with warmth.

Let's make this exercise easier. Read the five positive traits you just wrote down or thought about. What do you feel? It's very possible that you might not feel anything. You might shrug your shoulders and think that these qualities are standard, not so special or are dwarfed by those immense negative ones.

Did you write down 'Kind' as your positive trait? Imagine someone being kind to you. Imagine that you are in deep pain and crying alone. Your best friend swings by, sits next to you, warmly embraces you and soothes you until your tears dry out. Would you consider this act of kindness nothing? Would you tell your best friend, look, your kindness is not a big deal? I'm guessing you wouldn't. So why on earth would you say this to yourself? Think about it.

The negative double standard we treat ourselves with hurts us so often on a daily basis, we don't even realize it. We habitually downplay our positive traits in a way we'd never downplay others. And even worse, we punish ourselves for our shortcomings much more severely than we'd ever dare with others. We are the strictest with ourselves; we have the highest expectations for ourselves and the lowest level of understanding, compassion and tolerance towards ourselves.

Bobby didn't know that what he said was hurtful to me. Oh, well, I'm sure he didn't mean to harm me. He just doesn't know better. Why do we excuse Bobby? Why can't we just do the same thing with ourselves? *I didn't know that what I said was hurtful. Oh, well, I didn't mean to harm. I just didn't know better... And now that I know, I will apologize and I won't repeat the mistake.* Why can't we do just that?

What do we—usually—do instead? *Oh, why couldn't you just keep your ignorant, stupid mouth shut? You hurt Bobby. See? Are you satisfied? I always tell you how ignorant and dumb you are and that you'd better just listen and not talk. Now you did it. He is upset. And it's all your fault.* There is no acquittal, no self-compassion, just pure self-loathing. What do you think Bobby would do if you reacted to his mistake as you would react to your own? He'd probably get upset, feel attacked disproportionately and in the end he'd feel that he received a greater injustice than the one he caused. Also, he likely wouldn't want to be your friend anymore. What kind of person treats their friend with such an unforgiving, nasty attitude?

Yes, if you can relate by any means to my stories on negative self-talk, now's the time to realize that you aren't your own friend; not with such a negative double standard. You are not your own friend—

consequently, you wouldn't treat yourself with the grace of effort (to change) as you might treat a friend.

Befriend yourself. Treat yourself as you'd treat your favorite person in the world. Am I exaggerating? No, not at all. Be kind to yourself. This doesn't mean that you should turn a blind eye to your mistakes. But for crying out loud, you don't have to punish yourself like a 10th-century ascetic priest who just dropped the altar wine. When you make a mistake, think about how you would talk about that mistake if your friend made it. Certainly, you should tell your friend about it. Good friends help each other grow and growth often comes from realizing and admitting mistakes. How would you start the conversation? Likely with a statement that reassures your friend that he has your love and respect. "I value your friendship a lot..." or "I look up to you in..." or "I know that you highly appreciate honesty..." Then comes the *but* part, primed by a non-hostile attitude that lets your friend know that you mean well.

Do the same to yourself. Did you fall back into an old habit that you're working hard to overcome? Tell yourself that you acknowledge how much you do to overcome this habit, that you appreciate your own efforts and that you are aware of human imperfection. Then analyze the situation as it happened—what triggered your negative response, where did you lose track of your self-awareness, how could you have handled this issue differently? Come up with a few alternatives on how you'll deal with similar problems in the future. Take responsibility, say sorry, offer the option of restitution to the hurt party and try your best to make up for the mistake. Done. No further martyrdom is needed. You did the right thing. The people you hurt don't want you to mentally whip yourself until you're bleeding. And if they do, they are not well-wishers and you should stay away from them.

At the end of the day, the escape of the vicious cycle of self-blame also boils down to awareness and empathy; only in this case these are self-directed. Notice when you start whipping yourself with thoughts you wouldn't whip your loved ones with. This brief noticing creates a bit of space between you and your thoughts. Use this space to think about what you would tell a friend if they were the wrongdoer and empathetically apply your discoveries to yourself.

Journal Mode

Let's see how you can use your journal to productively explore your habits about blaming others and yourself.

1. **How do you stop blaming others?**

1. Awareness:

As we discussed in this chapter, the essence of changing our blaming habits is awareness. *A-ha* moments that arise in your mind will quickly fade away unless you write them down. This is why you have a journal.

Pick a specific event when you didn't own your

mistake, couldn't handle your anger, and blamed someone else instead. (Analyzing your general habits through specific events grants a deeper understanding in my experience. If we take a general look at the issue, it's harder to see cause-effect correlations, empathize and find helpful solutions. Let's just say it needs different lenses and fixes when you get impatient in the queue at the supermarket and you lash out at the slow cashier versus when you get impatient and lash out at your spouse after they fail to validate the great effort you put into cleaning the house. So be specific.)

Take a story from your recent past where you know you wronged someone. Collect all the ideas you can come up with about the situation. The most important parts are:

- What triggered the bad behavior?
- Where were you when the bad behavior happened?
- When did the bad behavior happen? Is this a solitary event or does it come up repetitively? Does it occur around the same time?

- Who were you with when your bad behavior was triggered?
- What emotions did you feel before, during and after the bad behavior?
- Why was your reaction exaggerated, malicious, hurtful, etc?
- What's your earliest memory of giving this reaction?
- Who gave the same or similar reactions in your childhood? Who did you learn this behavior from?

If you have any other ideas about your bad reaction, please add them here. If in time you gain new layers of awareness regarding this specific bad reaction, add them to your journal on a post-it. Take some time to compare your new revelations and ideas to the old ones and assess how much your understanding has improved. This kind of comparison is a good measurer of personal improvement and change.

Take a good, deep look at your answers. These are the 'signs' you need to catch before you engage in a reaction.

1. Empathy:

Now comes the second step: practicing empathy. Use the same story you did in the awareness part and now try to find answers to these questions:

- What would have I done, felt and thought in X's place?
- If X behaved the same way with me as I'm about to behave, how would I feel and react?
- Do I feel wronged by X? Is that why I plan to react poorly? Wasn't there any time in the past when I did the exact same thing X just did/said to me? How would I have liked to be treated in that case? Shouldn't I treat X the same way?
- Considering where X is coming from, how would I assess this situation? How would I react if I was X (who might see the problem from a different angle, who might not be emotionally involved as I am, etc.)?
- Instead of assuming the worst, what's the best I can assume about X's actions that triggered me?

Answer these questions honestly. I know it is difficult to step away from your righteousness. Try to do it.

This other person is another human being who is trying their best in their own reality.

1. Alternative responses:

The most important part of this journaling section is the active seeking of alternative responses. This step needs a little bit of extra work. The prerequisite of finding the best alternative answers depends on two things:

- What kind of person do your want to be?

- What kind of outcome (reward) do you seek in the situation?

Answer these two questions first. You know, the more you close the gap between your current self and your ideal self, the better you'll feel about yourself. That's just how it is. You need to be aware of who you want to be in order to create a new, more satisfying habitual pattern that overwrites the old one.

The second question, what outcome (reward) you expect from the interaction (your habitual response), is given for a long time. Essentially, your entire habit loop formed around the craving for that reward. Dig deep to find your true expectations for which you practice the bad habit. Sometimes we need to dig as far as early childhood to find the answer to this question. Who did you try to please/keep at a distance as a kid? Did you pretend to be someone you weren't to please your emotionally distant father? Were you screaming and rejecting, or utterly silent to stay safe from your alcoholic mother? What reward were you seeking? Safety? Love? Tension release?

What outcome are you looking for when you react? Does your reaction bring you the desired outcome?

I know I give you a lot to think about and an immense amount of questions to answer. There is no shortcut to this one, sorry. You created a lot of false beliefs and these were ruining your life for... only you know for how long. There's no abracadabra option—just hard, honest contemplation.

Once you answer all these questions, you can start to design alternative answers that align with your ideal self and that will truly bring you the outcome you want.

As a starter, write down three alternative responses you could give in similar cases. Make sure to think about how each of these responses would make the other person feel and what outcome they would generate.

1. **How do you stop your self-directed negativity?**

Time to fix your friendship with yourself. How do you fix a friendship that has been broken? By first sucking out the poison. Just as you would approach a friend whom you hurt badly, approach yourself with an honest apology.

1. Apologize:

Write down at least five things in your journal about how you wronged yourself and say sorry for them.

I know I did a lot of damage when I said you could never change. I was wrong and caged you into a false belief, making your life miserable. I'm sorry, please forgive me.

I know, it's a bit crazy to talk to yourself like that. But hey, you talk to yourself all day anyway. Now at least you're telling yourself something uplifting and liberating. Apologize to your hurt self and forgive yourself. Self-absolution is a quiet room with a beam of light.

1. Empower:

After you have acknowledged at least five things you harmed yourself with and apologized for them, write down (if you didn't do so already) your five strengths. And additionally, contemplate about why and how those qualities bring goodness in the world.

If you already stepped onto the path of change and you received some good feedback on your efforts, write them down swiftly. This is the real proof that you are able to change and that you are a much better person than you think.

For example, I discovered that for a long time, out of a victim mentality, I took many people's help for granted without showing sufficient (or any) gratitude. My first big act after this realization was to write an apology letter (physical or email) to every single person I could recall who helped me and I didn't appreciate the gesture from properly. These letters included people such as my cheating ex-boyfriend, my ever-so-critical aunt, and my always-rejecting brother. It was freaking hard to write those letters and be empathetic with them as I received scars from these people. But I also gave scars to them. And for the scars I gave, I was responsible.

As a result, I rekindled the relationship with my brother. We both told each other our stories. He told me why he was so distant with me, deep-rooted family issues I didn't know about. We share a father but have different mothers. My mother's schizophrenic delirium and my father's lack of assertiveness and protection chased away my brother from our home, leaving deep scars and fear in him. He is almost forty years old now and I never knew about his pain. We connected. We forgave and asked for forgiveness. It was a beautiful experience.

My ex-boyfriend had his side of the story regarding our relationship and his own share of childhood traumas that led him to be as he was. I failed to see this side of him before. I was boiling in my petty rage. My hurt ego witch-hunted him for almost ten years.

A few days ago we talked, and freed each other from the darkness of our past. It felt extremely liberating. He still won't be within the top five people on my friends list but I can see and accept where he is coming from and what shaped him in his life. We share a lot of scars and behavioral problems—being together, these just got magnified, which made us a bad match, not bad people.

My aunt graciously accepted my letter and gifts I sent her and assured me that on her side there were no hard feelings. She knew that I was young and immature so she didn't take my lack of gratitude personally. She feels, however, very good now that her efforts are recognized.

Feedback like this gives you that nudge you need to feel more positive and proud about yourself. To me the 'hate myself-love myself' transition was a collection of little positive feedbacks that followed me doing the (scary but) right thing. Slowly I noticed that the presence of the negative voice in my head lessened. Then I noticed that a positive voice started lecturing the negative whenever it tried its luck and blamed me harshly again. These days I feel very proud of myself and of who I have become in such a short time.

I still have my low points and the negative self-talk still tries to contaminate my brain but now I just think, *Oh, here you are. I was sure you'd show up in a moment like this. Now please stay silent while the adult one (me) is thinking. Thanks.* And I continue my journaling analysis I presented to you in this chapter under bullet point A. The negative voice gets tired of waiting and slowly dissolves.

Keep in mind one thing: your negative self-talk thrives on your attention. If you ignore it consciously, it has no chance of survival.

Negative emotions and thoughts are just like the mud at the bottom of an otherwise crystal clear lake. Sometimes when something enters the lake, the mud gets whirled up making the lake look dirty. Trying to get rid of the mud floating on the water by pushing it down won't work. The more you push the mud, the more it will break onto the surface. But if you just let the mud be by acknowledging it but not touching it, slowly it will settle at the bottom of the lake.

So allow yourself to be a bit muddy occasionally. Don't forget your five virtues in the meantime and collect as much positive feedback as you can about your change. By the way, positive feedback doesn't have to be external. When you handle an argument successfully with your new alternative response, and get the outcome you desire, that's also a big fat victory that should be immediately put into your journal. It has maybe an even bigger self-love boosting potential than external feedback. Empower yourself.

1. Empathize:

Did you mess up? Who doesn't? Stay kind to yourself. When you collect a healthy amount of self-love and respect, I tell you through experience that negative self-talk will not come up as your go-to reaction to your mistake. As crazy as it sounds, when you don't lack self-love and respect, being negative with yourself won't feel satisfying anymore. You won't feel fulfilled by lecturing yourself in an ugly manner—what you'll crave will be a solution, a fix, a lesson that follows the mess-up. You'll value your life and time, so spending several minutes or hours with a failure without gaining something good from it won't feel like a productive, time-worthy option anymore. Getting there, though, is not a two-day project. It takes a lot of mindfulness, effort and time. But it's not impossible, so roll your sleeves up and work hard to get there.

In the meantime, practice the "How would I treat my friend in this case?" method to show yourself empathy. Did you mess up? Write down in your journal how you would handle this mistake if your friend committed it. What would you tell them? What advice would you give? Then apply these answers to yourself.

Additionally, feel some empathy for your tired brain and body. It's very hard to keep a new habit in your conscious mind when you feel exhausted or sad. Don't excuse yourself for the bad behavior but soothe yourself nevertheless. You have finite willpower and energy—keep that in mind and stop expecting perfection from yourself. Make sure to take responsibility, apologize and make up for your mistake when you feel more rested.

Give yourself the grace to see yourself as a human being with limitations, as someone who is working hard to be a better person. That's the best, and all you can do.

Finally, write down words of gratitude to yourself.

I'm grateful for keeping it together today when my husband stepped on my triggers. I'm grateful that I was able to overcome my fear of rejection and complimented a stranger.

You get it. Now, time to stop reading and start writing.

Complimentary Journal for Chapter 2:

a.) My 5 weaknesses or things I don't like about myself:

----

b.) My 5 strengths or things I love about myself (make sure to not choose what others like about you but what you do):

Complimentary Journal for Chapter 2:

____

____

____

____

____

c.) How to stop blaming others?

1. Awareness

Pick a specific event when you didn't own your mistake, couldn't handle your anger, and blamed someone else instead.

Event #1:

____

____

Now collect all the ideas you can come up with about the situation. The most important parts are:

- What triggered the bad behavior?

____

____

- Where were you when the bad behavior happened?

____

____

- When did the bad behavior happen? Is this a solitary event or does it come up repetitively? Does it occur around the same time?

____

____

- Who were you with when your bad behavior was triggered?

____

____

- What emotions did you feel before, during and after the bad behavior?

____

____

- Why was your reaction exaggerated, malicious, hurtful, etc?

- What's your earliest memory of giving this reaction?

- Who gave the same or similar reactions in your childhood? Who did you learn this behavior from?

If you have any other ideas about your bad reaction, please add them here. If in time you gain new layers of awareness regarding this specific bad reaction, add it to your journal on a post it.

- My idea:

____

____

- My idea:

____

____

____

- My idea:

____

____

____

Event #2:

____

____

Now collect all the ideas you can come up with about the situation. The most important parts are:

- What triggered the bad behavior?

____

____

- Where were you when the bad behavior happened?

____

____

- When did the bad behavior happen? Is this a solitary event or does it come up repetitively? Does it occur around the same time?

____

____

- Who were you with when your bad behavior was triggered?

____

____

- What emotions did you feel before, during and after the bad behavior?

____

____

- Why was your reaction exaggerated, malicious, hurtful, etc?

____

____

- What's your earliest memory of giving this reaction?

____

____

- Who gave the same or similar reactions in your childhood? Who did you learn this behavior from?

If you have any other ideas about your bad reaction, please add them here. If in time you gain new layers of awareness regarding this specific bad reaction, add it to your journal on a post it.

- My idea:

- My idea:

- My idea:

____

____

____

Event #3:

____

____

Now collect all the ideas you can come up with about the situation. The most important parts are:

- What triggered the bad behavior?

____

____

- Where were you when the bad behavior happened?

____

____

- When did the bad behavior happen? Is this a solitary event or does it come up repetitively? Does it occur around the same time?

____

____

- Who were you with when your bad behavior was triggered?

____

____

- What emotions did you feel before, during and after the bad behavior?

____

____

- Why was your reaction exaggerated, malicious, hurtful, etc?

____

____

- What's your earliest memory of giving this reaction?

____

____

- Who gave the same or similar reactions in your childhood? Who did you learn this behavior from?

____

____

If you have any other ideas about your bad reaction, please add them here. If in time you gain new layers of awareness regarding this specific bad reaction, add it to your journal on a post it.

- My idea:

____

____

____

- My idea:

____

____

____

- My idea:

____

____

____

Take some time to compare your new revelations and ideas to the old ones and assess how much your understanding has improved. This kind of comparison is a good measurer of personal improvement and change.

2. Empathy.

Now comes the second step: practicing empathy. Answer the upcoming questions honestly. I know it is difficult but try to do it. Remember that this other person is another human being who is trying their best in their own reality.

Use the same story you did in the awareness part and now try to find answers to these questions:

Event #1:

____

____

- What would have I done, felt and thought in X's place?

____

____

- If X behaved the same way with me as I'm about to behave, how would I feel and react?

____

____

- Do I feel wronged by X? Is that why I plan to react poorly? Wasn't there any time in the past when I did the exact same thing X just did/said to me? How would I have liked to be treated in that case? Shouldn't I treat X the same way?

____

____

____

____

- Considering where X is coming from, how would I assess this situation? How would I react if I was X (who might see the problem from a different angle, who might not be emotionally involved as I am, etc.)?

____

____

____

____

- Instead of assuming the worst, what's the best I can assume about X's actions that triggered me?

____

____

Event #2:

____

____

- What would have I done, felt and thought in X's place?

____

____

- If X behaved the same way with me as I'm about to behave, how would I feel and react?

____

____

- Do I feel wronged by X? Is that why I plan to react poorly? Wasn't there any time in the past when I did the exact same thing X just did/said to me? How would I have liked to be treated in that case? Shouldn't I treat X the same way?

____

____

____

____

- Considering where X is coming from, how would I assess this situation? How would I react if I was X (who might see the problem from a different angle, who might not be emotionally involved as I am, etc.)?

____

____

- Instead of assuming the worst, what's the best I can assume about X's actions that triggered me?

Event #3:

- What would have I done, felt and thought in X's place?

- If X behaved the same way with me as I'm about to behave, how would I feel and react?

- Do I feel wronged by X? Is that why I plan to react poorly? Wasn't there any time in the past when I did the exact same thing X just did/said to me? How would I have liked to be treated in that case? Shouldn't I treat X the same way?

- Considering where X is coming from, how would I assess this situation? How would I react if I was X (who might see the problem from a different angle, who might not be emotionally involved as I am, etc.)?

- Instead of assuming the worst, what's the best I can assume about X's actions that triggered me?

----

3. Alternative responses.

What kind of person do I want to be? (Write down at least eight attributives.)

____

____

____

____

____

Does my reaction bring me the desired outcome I am seeking in the analyzed events?

What outcome am I looking for when I react in:

Event #1:

____

____

____

____

Event #2:

____

____

Event #3:

Dig deep to find your true expectations for which you practice the bad habit. Sometimes we need to dig as far as early childhood to find the answer to this question. Who did you try to please/keep at a distance as a kid? Did you pretend to be someone you weren't to please your emotionally distant father? Were you screaming and rejecting, or utterly silent to stay safe from your alcoholic mother? What reward were you seeking? Safety? Love? Tension release?

d.) Start to design alternative answers that align with your ideal self and will truly bring you the outcome you want. Write down three alternative responses you could give in the analyzed events. (Make sure to think about how each of these responses would make the other person feel and what outcome would they generate.)

Event #1:

1.

____

____

____

____

2.

____

____

____

____

3.

____

____

____

____

Event #2:

1.

____

____

____

____

2.

____

____

____

____

3.

____

____

____

____

Event #3:

1.

____

____

____

____

2.

____

____

____

____

3.

____

----

e.) How to stop your self-directed negativity?

1. Apologize to yourself. Write down at least five things in your journal how you wronged yourself and say sorry for them.

Apology #1:

Apology #2:

____

Apology #3:

____

____

____

____

Apology #4:

____

____

____

____

Apology #5:

____

____

____

____

2. Empower. Recall your 5 strengths from point b.). Contemplate about why and how those qualities bring goodness in the world.

Strength #1:

____

____

____

____

Strength #2:

____

____

____

____

Strength #3:

____

____

____

____

Strength #4:

____

____

____

____

Strength #5:

____

____

____

____

3. Empathize. Did you mess up? Write down in your journal how you would handle this mistake if your friend committed it. What would you tell them? What advice would you give? Then apply these answers to yourself.

Blooper #1:

____

____

____

____

____

____

____

____

Blooper #2:

____

____

____

____

____

____

____

____

Blooper #3:

____

____

____

____

____

____

____

____

f.) Write down words of gratitude to yourself.

Dear ______, I'm grateful for you for:

____

____

____

____

____

Untitled

3

Step Three: Forged in Pain

It was a tough lesson. I sat on a plane, traveling to the island of Langkawi, Malaysia, listening to this audiobook that I bought to learn and understand more the relationship with my father. My heart felt joyful as I imagined how this book would unveil the imperfections of my father, talking about his mistakes in an eloquently scientific language I couldn't use myself, explaining point by point how guilty and messed up he was and would then give me a green card for my own behavior. *With the father (and mother) you had, no wonder you turned out to be as you are, poor baby*. For sure, the book provided me with this affirmation but it didn't give me the green card I hoped for.

The more I progressed with my listening, the more my attention drifted from identifying the message with my father to identifying it with myself. It was a terrifying, first-in-a-lifetime realization: I'm not much different or better than him.

All my life, all of it, I was deluding myself with the belief that since I disliked his way of *being* so much, it was impossible that I'd become anything like him. On a surface level I was different. Unlike him, I was hardworking, obsessively keeping my promises, faithful to my partner, I felt responsible for those very few people I let get close to me and I let them go extremely hard. But I was also impatient, self-centered, mean, snappy, superficial in my values, quick to argue but shy to seek solutions, I didn't know what saying sorry or taking responsibility meant, being truly empathetic, I was choking on a sense of entitlement—I felt that for some inexplicable but undeniable reason I was special and better than others; just like him. There is a saying in Hungary, "The empty spica holds its head the highest," meaning that those who know the least tend to be the most proud; well, my father and I were just the most eloquent example of this saying.

The more I listened to my audiobook, the less I could

think about my father in its context. I was stunned by the realization this book gave me. You know the cliché about a book changing your life? I can attest that this cliché is true to the core in my case. This book indeed changed my life. After I finished listening, memories invaded my brain; older relatives who tried to warn me about my flaws in character, guys who chose to not put up with me and I was puzzled why, guys who put up with me but often mentioned similar things as the book, which I brushed off, annoyed. *This is who I am. I can't change. I won't. My dad taught me not to give in to people who try to make me be someone I'm not. My dad taught me not to let anyone step on me.* All these attempts to warn, help and save me from myself came back to me in an eerie cacophony. I felt overwhelmed and confused. Finally, I opened up to my partner about my discoveries. He was happy that I finally 'got it'. But soon he became very angry and disappointed with me for putting him through so much trouble in the past three and a half years we've been together.

Shit like this isn't pretty.

You get all these realizations about yourself, how wrong you were about some things, how much you need to fix and heal, and you don't even know where to find solid ground in your melting personality; your faith in your knowledge that you mindlessly projected into the world became relative and questionable. Your love of three and a half years with whom your previous deluded self thought everything was awesome with—had even planned to marry him soon—suddenly tells you that you have never actually been a good partner and that he seriously plans on leaving you... If I called this state of being a low point it would be an understatement.

I know that Hollywood movies sell you the idea that this is the point where you graciously rise like in Bonnie Tyler's *I need a Hero*, defeat all the odds and become the redeemed champion of your tale. I want to tell you that I did just that.

Nope. I didn't.

Instead I wept and wept for weeks, feeling sorry for myself; feeling abandoned, rejected and injured. I was angry with my boyfriend that he didn't support me in a time like this and instead turned his back, selfishly demanding *his* pain to be addressed now. "His pain? What about my pain? My entire life was a lie," I grumbled to myself. I didn't get it. I couldn't get it at that point. I didn't see that while he was hurt, he was still with me, he still listened to my endless crying about my pain, he still sent me links, books and articles that may help me. I was still self-absorbed, still felt entitled to mother-like soothing affections. *It's okay, little Zoe, you are still my perfect child.* I desperately wanted to be excused, to be let off the hook, to be away from the pain.

I failed to see that although I was able to understand there was a problem with me, I still looked at myself and the world with those same old eyes, and took actions led by the same old habits. My foolish pride led me to believe that by listening to that one book I understood three decades of misbehavior and now I could become better if people would just get over themselves, see how much *I* suffer, and lend me a hand.

I so wish to tell you that knowledge only is enough to turn your ship around; that it can kick your life in a better direction, that with some knowledge and willpower you can 'fake it 'til you make it' in a pain-less environment. Nope, that wasn't true for me. My case needed as much pain as it could get to steer the wheels of change for good. My selfish, old self was desperately floundering in me, trying its best to survive for a long time.

I was curious by nature so I kept reading books—Brene Brown's *The Power of Vulnerability, Daring Greatly, The Gifts of Imperfection*; James Altucher's *Reinvent Yourself*; Pema Chödrön's *When Things Fall Apart, Start Where You Are*; Desmond Tutu's *Book of Forgiving*; Gary Chapman and Jennifer Thomas's *When Sorry Isn't Enough*; and Eckhart Tolle's *The Power of Now* just to name a few. Day and night I was listening to books and podcasts, reading blogs and Reddit feeds. I got more and more knowledge—and more and more pride.

Oh boy, now I'm so well equipped on how to be a decent human being like never before. *What can go wrong when you read and understand so much?*

The more time passed, the more I read, and the more my pain deepened. My boyfriend was very angry with me still, didn't even touch me and hardly looked at me. My biggest confidant since forever, my father, was the last person I wanted to talk to. By nature I didn't want to bother my friends with my problems—another silly part of me, assuming that my friends would not want me if I opened up more about my 'dark side'. I was alone. Like capital-A alone. I often cried for no apparent reason. Some days I woke up with a hopeful, even cheerful attitude and went meditating at a nearby park. On other days I felt as miserable as a turkey in November, terrified that my boyfriend would dump me. I was terrified of myself. When will my 'old self' break through my fragile shield and make another mistake, another defensive outburst, and ruin all my hard work? What if I can't change quickly enough *for him*? What if I can't change at all? What if he leaves me? What if I will be left by everyone for the rest of my life? Am I a bad person? How bad am I? Do I deserve... anything?

Thoughts like these were the 24/7 radio program in my head that I tried to silence with loud, positivity-spouting audiobooks. No way would I have touched a physical book in that period. Something had to go in my head, otherwise I feared I'd go legitimately nuts.

And then, in the middle of this insanity came Andrea, my therapist, and her life-changing recommendation of keeping a journal which helps keep order in my thought-jungle. It worked.

As time passed, thanks to the books I consumed, Andrea and my excessive journaling work, my internal world slowly started shifting. The more I understood concepts that previously were foreign in practice like empathy, taking responsibility, the importance of saying sorry, the strong influence of shame that often prevented me from even thinking about the many things I lacked, the even stronger influence of ignorance, pride and entitlement, the more humbled I became.

I couldn't pinpoint what exactly triggered my slow drift away from my self-centeredness to more distant perspectives. It must have happened while journaling. One thing I know and that I'm sure of is that this switch was forged in pain. My pain led me to keep reading when I felt things were falling apart. My pain made me sit down day after day to meditate for half an hour when I knew, just knew, that my efforts were doomed. My pain made me seek better and better solutions to get what I wanted. Beneath my egotistical false self, my real self felt my pain and helped me. At the end of the day my personal, greatest life change was not happening thanks to more knowledge, or thanks to more diligence or even thanks to more understanding. It was thanks to that overwhelming pain I felt and wished to escape. Just like an animal in distress, I was running towards what I perceived as safe. There was nothing glorious about it, nothing Hollywood-movie-like. In the beginning my subconscious mind tried to run back to its old habits as that was what felt safe to it in that period. But thanks to the pain generated by my cognitive dissonance, the growing threat of my love leaving me, the silent fear that I will end up like my father after all—proud and alone—I understood: I can't go back to where I come from. There is no safe place in my 'old self'. There never was, but back then I didn't know that—now I do. So I can't go back there, no matter what.

Where could I go then? What was safe? Silence. I got no answer from within. So my soul just ran and ran, discovering new territories, looking for solutions like it never did before, skills I previously thought I didn't have, actions that I previously thought I was not designed to do. The deeper I dug in my journaling practice, the more that walls built on lies started to crumble.

The process of change was as simple and as hard as that.

Days turned into weeks, weeks into months—the calendar year changed. In this time I made more discoveries about the world, friends, family and myself than in my previous three decades altogether. No school taught me these things. Books helped, the therapist helped, my loved ones helped (sometimes with tough love) but I had to make these discoveries myself. I had to do the grind myself. I had to stomach my flaws alone. I had to forgive myself... That's a tough one.

You know, the interesting part of self-discovery is that every time you invest a lot of thought and time into it and arrive to a conclusion, you think you've got it figured out. *Now I know what was wrong, what I should do and how I can become better.* Then you talk to someone, read something, think more empathetically and there you go: your fragile sense of self and baby belief system is down again.

Sometimes I imagine that all (or most) of the walls built on lies that I constructed in my life are down now. There is a desolate city which just got trashed by an earthquake. Every time I think I understand something, I start building a new house on the ruins. Every time this understanding gets overwritten, the house crumbles. In other words, every time I achieve some success with my understanding, I become cocky and laidback, believing that the hard work is behind me now. Then life proves me wrong. Bang. Pleasure is not a good advisor, you see.

Today, I don't build anything anymore. I just sit on the ruins. I own them. They are my responsibility, *my* ruins. It's my responsibility to keep people safe from these ruins but it's also my responsibility to cherish and love them as they are the pavements I'm sitting on today. Without those ruins I wouldn't be who I am today. I need no house for my soul. No house, no walls. I want to feel grateful when the sunshine touches my heart but I also want to feel the rain because that's what waters my personal growth.

One of the key takeaways of my self-discovery journey so far is also one of the hardest to practice: welcoming the pain. Every successful person whose articles, books and memoirs I read have this message in common: failure, pain and hardship will help you grow. These are the elemental powers that drift even the darkest mind to improvement.

The other essential ingredient besides fear is just a little wish to change, just a little acknowledgement of one's undeniable flaws. If pain and a slight wish for change is given, the process will catch snowball-effect-like momentum and sooner or later it will break through habitual resistance.

Both pain and the wish for change needs to be present. Without pain, even if you wish to change, it's much harder to take steps towards and consolidate the desired change. I have never met a person who was absolutely fulfilled yet worked hard on changing. There has to be some dissatisfaction with the status quo that generates some form of pain, and that can kick even the luckiest men on earth towards change.

If there is no will and acknowledgement that change is needed, one can be burning in the proverbial hell of pain but won't change. Why would someone want to change just because they feel pain when they think there is nothing wrong with *them*? Of course, they want something to change; their mom, their partner, maybe the economy. The entire world should change to soothe their pain. What about changing themselves? No way. It's not *their fault* this is happening. My father has a similar mindset—he dismisses the possibility that his misfortunes are, at the end of the day, his doings. He rejects that they are his responsibility to deal with.

One fundamental mistake people like my dad make is that they confuse fault with responsibility. Just because something is not their fault, it doesn't mean that their interpretation or reaction to the problem is not their responsibility. Conversely, people often dread to take responsibility because they believe that this automatically puts the blame on them; they become at fault. They end up avoiding both fault and responsibility to stay 'safe' while getting consumed by the pain and not understanding why.

I know this problem too well as I lived in it for so long. How could I escape it? Honestly? I will put it plainly.

I had to admit to myself that I was wrong about how I behaved and how I made people feel most of my life. Most. Of. My. Life. And then I had to eat a lot of shit. That's right. I had to be mindful about not reverting to my old defenses where nothing was my fault or my responsibility. I had to own up to my mistakes made in those years when I should have taken responsibility but didn't.

I still have to swallow occasionally the consequences of my past blindness and lack of awareness. Not only in the form of feedback I get from people who I wounded in some way, but also from myself. What do I mean by this? I mean that what to others may be second nature (being a good listener, empathetic, quick on apologizing and taking responsibility), to me they are a constant dread. Not because these actions make me feel bad—they actually make me feel much better about myself and happier. But at the same time they are very unnatural for my brain to execute them. I have to be very present when I engage in a discussion with someone as I can easily revert to my old habits before I realize it. This kind of hypervigilance is exhausting and makes life feel artificial, uncomfortable and ultimately painful.

But this is a different kind of pain, the one you feel when you do the right thing even though it is not a habitual response yet; a much lighter and more rewarding pain than the one you feel when you mess something up big time and try putting out fires that would have been avoidable. This is the pain of the discomfort of doing, not the pain of shame, regret, remorse, anger or other negative emotions. Making a conscious choice to act against your old habits is never natural at first, but in this phase of change our goal (our reward) is not to do something that feels natural.

The goal is the choice: to be present and conscious enough to think about the fact that we have a choice. Habitual reactions don't require a choice or awareness; they come regardless. In this sense, in the early stages of change, familiarity, 'the natural', is the enemy. Pain and discomfort are the friends.

These days I have learned to appreciate and feel grateful for discomfort and pain. They mean I'm on the right track. Whenever I feel that a thought got through my filter way too easily, I double-check it. *Why did this happen? Where is my discomfort?* Thought policing, while practically unsustainable in the long run, is very helpful in the early phases of changing your behavior. It helps not only catch old-habit-created thoughts but also helps establish new habits. Some thoughts go through our filter easier because the adoption process of the new, good habitual behavior has gotten more grounded in our psyche. This observation is the best we can make in the early phase of change. When through thought policing we catch more and more thoughts that are generated by our new mental habits, the more empowered we'll feel about being on the right track.

For example, previously when I considered my boyfriend's complaints, I assessed them from an angle of self-centeredness. *How can I make his pain go away so he stops nagging me?* Where was my focus? On my pain. Ever since my self-discovery journey started I wished to change this kind of thinking. So for months I made a conscious effort to be more empathetic and consider his pain from his perspective every time he had something to share.

Oh, man, it was difficult. In the early days I couldn't help but drift back to becoming defensive and losing focus of his needs. One day I listened to his complaints and addressed them in a way he found satisfying. And I found it effortless. I instantly became suspicious of myself. *How come? Usually I can keep it together like this at the cost of so much self-control. This was way too easy. Did I deceive him or myself?* After a long analysis in my journal I concluded that no, I was honest about what I said and I honestly felt that I wanted him to be happy so badly. That was the first moment when I felt that all the tears, the months spent in anguish, in discomfort and with Spartan mental discipline were not in vain; moreover, it was all worth the pain. We finally made a real connection; an honest and vulnerable one. This was a connection of our true selves, not a fabricated one boosted on serotonin that we felt in our early days of love.

The connection you make with your bare, vulnerable self, funnily enough, is not really about you. It's more about acknowledging and embracing another being's bare vulnerability which is different than yours but just as real and precious.

I'm sitting in a park right now. As I write this chapter I can't help but think that I'm fine. I'm in more control than I have ever been before. I feel good about who I am. Not crazy good, I just feel fine. I give in to the gentle sensation of the wind on my face. I enjoy it. I recall that only a few months ago I sat in the same park; confused, broken, full of self-resentment, drowning in hopelessness and self-pity. Back then I thought I would never feel good again, because if someone lived in the darkness of their mind for so long, it would be impossible to break out. I thought that maybe there was nothing else left—just that darkness and the awareness of it. I was even debating whether or not knowing about the darkness was truly better than being ignorant. *For sure, the knowledge hasn't made my life better so far. Quite the opposite, I have never felt so miserable even on the worst days of my oblivious existence.*

Today, I know that:

- The book *Adult Children of Emotionally Immature Parents* was the best thing that ever happened to me as it opened my eyes;
- The painful cognitive dissonance that followed this newfound knowledge was the most necessary thing that ever happened to me, as without it I wouldn't have made active steps to change;
- The sometimes tearful—sometimes hopeless—transition period was the most just thing that ever happened to me as it taught me to understand the consequences of my actions and then take responsibility for them; and
- The self-respect and self-love I feel today is the most fulfilling gift I ever received as it tells me that the path I'm on is good; not only for me but also for everyone around me

Self-fulfillment and self-love counterintuitively come to you when you give back. There is a common saying that you can't give what you don't have. In other words, you can't love others unless you love yourself. This is partially true but it doesn't mean that you can't build up self-love through being loving to others. Harville Hendrix, Ph.D. explains why this is in his book *Getting The Love You Want.* It depends on an external stimulus, after all, but not as we usually seek it.

When we are able to overcome our inner resistance and satisfy others' needs—be it a romantic partner, a friend or parents—a part of our conscious mind interprets the caring behavior as self directed. "Love of the self is achieved through the love of the other," Hendrix explains. To understand why the psyche works this way, we need to know something about our old, reptilian brain. "The old brain doesn't know that the outside world exists. Instead it responds to the impulses generated by the cerebral cortex. Lacking a direct connection to the external world, the old brain assumes that all behavior is inner directed. When you are able to become more generous and loving to your spouse therefore your old brain assumes that this activity is intended for you."[1]

Technically, it doesn't matter with whom we start to act nicely towards—others or ourselves—our old brain will still interpret it as self-love. While you don't get fulfilled by craving, and getting, validation from others, you get fulfilled by validating yourself through giving wholeheartedly to others. Others are needed in your self-fulfillment and self-love journey but their validation will not help you achieve it. Your own actions will.

To adopt this conclusion will take some time and effort. As I mentioned before, you will face some serious setbacks. You will repeat old mistakes often, especially in the beginning. You will question different things daily: your past self, the usefulness of this new knowledge, your ability to change, your worth and the worth of the people around you. Just put in the effort, friend. Just be honest with yourself and know who you want to be.

You will feel that you are not in control. Haunting events, emotions and past demons will show up in your mind randomly. One day you'll feel that you made progress. The next day you'll wake up like a total mess and you'll pray this entire process had never started. The next day you'll feel okay again and chill a bit—and you'll repeat an old mistake. The next day you'll resent yourself for not being better by now with all that knowledge and all the practice you did. Then the next day you'll resent your previous day's self-resentment. You'll meditate. You'll eat a lot one day and the next you'll feel you couldn't swallow a piece of rice even if it was forced into you. One day you'll crave company and harass all your friends. The next day you'll feel that you have no desire to speak to anyone. One day you'll spend constantly thinking about the causes and effects of your behavior development. Another day you'll live on an absolutely oblivious level wondering how it can be six in the evening already. You'll feel extreme stress and self-doubt sometimes. Other times you'll be self-assured and relaxed. The next day you'll be confused by how you can feel both states in the same day. Some days you'll feel that you're going crazy. Other days you'll think you're finally getting out of being crazy.

And on an ordinary day you'll sit on a bench in a park, noticing the mild breeze on your skin. You'll close your eyes, breathe in and out and feel at peace. You'll feel gratitude. All that will matter is that you are alive. You are one with the nature that surrounds you, one with everyone else. In those moments you won't feel alone. All the problems, stress, pain, self-doubt, self-confidence, joy, calmness and self-fulfillment will suddenly make sense, although you'll also know they don't make sense at all. And that's okay. You're okay.

Right now there is nothing—just you and the breeze. In this moment there are no problems. In this moment there is nothing to fix. Just be. Just live.

Journal Mode

Jean Piaget, the Swiss genius behind the theory of cognitive development, discovered that in order to learn new things, first we must break our old mental patterns and re-work them around the new, desired knowledge. This is the quintessential part of intellectual development. In this chapter I talked about pain being our ally in a process of change. Science backs me up on that statement. Piaget pinpointed that emotional distress can be a sign of growth which roots in the newly activated urge to grow.[1]

Another psychologist, the Polish Kazimierz Dabrowski, calls this process 'positive disintegration': We break our beliefs down to reorganize them and establish more emotionally complex feelings. He states that negative emotions are the motivators behind this psychological development.[2]

In this chapter's Journal Mode I will help you prove to yourself that pain helped and shaped you to be better much more than you previously gave credit for. If you haven't thought of the benefits of painful tragedies yet, let's do it now together. Becoming conscious of the benefits you received due to a painful experience is extremely important. This way you can decide to keep your focus on these benefits and use them as the means for growth in your 'positive disintegration' process.

Exercise 1: Gold in the Dust

Recall the five biggest failures or devastating moments of your life. They can be anything—a death in your family, a break up, a lost job. Choose a few recent events and a few older ones.

Think about them for a few moments and answer the following questions:

1. When this event happened I felt...
2. Six months after this event I felt...
3. Five years after this event I felt...
4. How did this event change my worldview? What did I learn from this event?

Honestly answering these questions can shed a light on how your feelings have changed over time even about the most relevant negative experiences in your life.

(If the painful event you chose is more recent than five years or six months, just answer points 1 (and 2, if applicable) and add the current time distance and feelings you have in relation to the event today.)

For example, my grandparents (who raised me) passed away twelve years ago.

1. When this event happened I felt... numb. I couldn't comprehend what their deaths meant. I had never lost anyone close to me before. I went to their funeral and accompanied them on their last journey. And I went on with my life. Thinking back

now, I repressed the pain of their loss very aggressively. What I thought I needed more in those times was sympathy from my peers for my loss rather than dealing with my loss.

1. Six months after my grandparents died, I was still in total pain repression mode. I thought about them often, I cried but I didn't open the door on my soul to think about what their loss truly meant. I was running away from blissful, happy memories with them like they were the plague. I refused, thinking about who would make me those delicious plum dumplings if not my grandma? Who would play chess with me if not my grandpa? Where will I spend my school holidays if not... *at home*? Looking back today, I can clearly see that I was in denial and isolation just like the five stages of grief predict.

Then my parents sold my grandparents' house... For some reason that was the moment when things sank in: my beloved mama and tata were really gone. I don't know why, but I became obsessed with that house. I was angry, protesting on a daily basis, begging my parents not to sell it. I cried to them one day, I yelled the next. I was mad—as if preserving the house would preserve them, too. A few days before the sale went through, we visited their house one last time. This was well beyond the one-year mark of their death. I entered the house I loved so much, the only place I considered home thus far or ever since. And I felt nothing. Empty. Nada. It was a shocking realization.

I learned an important lesson that day: People make places special. Without the people we love, even the 'best things in life' are empty. People we love are the gold in the dust called life.

1. Five years after the death of my grandparents, I missed them so much it hurt. Whatever warm memories my heart blocked out in the first year flooded me with full power in the next ones. I didn't think about them as often as in the first six months but when I did it was harrowing. I kept recalling the last time I saw my grandma sitting alone on her little bench. My grandpa had passed away just a few days ago. The once lively environment

> filled with lazy cats, cheerful dogs, clucking chickens, bright flowers, mellow grapes and lush green grass was gone. Her husband of 55 years was gone. I was gone—to Hungary for high school, hardly ever visiting them. She just sat there with glassy eyes that already looked dead, long before her actual death three months later. I so wish I could turn back time... to run to her, and tell her that I love her. That I'm so bloody grateful for her raising me, that she took care of me and that I appreciate every single sacrifice she made... (Damn, my tears started pouring as I'm typing this.)

Twelve years have passed and I still can't write about my regrets related to her without crying. When I recall that deep youthful ignorance and that fear of showing my love, it makes me feel so sorry.

God knows when I will be able to forgive myself for that. I hope soon, but at the same time I hope I never forget this feeling of regretful sorrow. I want to remember it so that I never make the same mistake again. This thought brings me to point 4.

1. *How did this event change my worldview? What did I learn from this event?*

Don't take life for granted. Neither yours nor those around you. Every trivial moment you spend with a loved one is a blessing which you will only understand once they are gone. If you had only one takeaway from this book, make it this:

- Tell your loved ones how you feel about them now. There might not be another chance;
- If you have a sense of awkwardness when you say "I love you", "I appreciate what you do for me" and "You are very important to me" to your loved ones, practice to overcome it. However awkward you may feel by saying these things doesn't compare to the power of the regret you'll feel once they're gone and you can't tell them these things anymore; and
- If you love your loved ones, show your love for Christ's sake. Pick up the phone, write that letter, wear that ugly sweater and eat that slightly salty cake made with love!

The scar of losing someone dear never heals—in my experience. But in time you'll get better. And even in sorrow like death there are valuable lessons that can help you grow as a person. 'Thanks' to losing my grandparents who raised me, I developed a very openly loving, affectionate side of me to my father, my mother and everyone I care about. It still feels awkward to say "I love you" but I say it anyway. Sometimes it is hard to keep in touch with my parents but I do it anyway. I shower them with selflessly selfish gestures—to show them my caring and to save myself from regret; to heal them and heal myself.

Take time to complete this exercise. Go to places you've never been before when you analyze the painful event in question. I presented a death as an example just to show you that there is plenty to learn and journal about something irreversibly devastating like that.

The events you choose to assess through these four points are legitimate painful memories. Not only cases of human loss apply. Did you lose your well-paying job two years ago and ever since you've been working for nickels and can't give your kids what you want? That's just as good an example and learning field as any. Did your husband run away with the yoga instructor? This pain requires quite a lot of journaling and you might need to dig deep for lessons. Do it. Now. Immerse yourself in that pain but in the end, focus on point 4, the lessons, and allow yourself to grow spiritually.

Exercise 2: Forgive Yourself like Your Life Depends on It

Pain is educational and helps us grow to become better people. Painful memories hold in themselves very important lessons we can use to improve. But—here comes the long awaited, proverbial *but*—no one wants to live in pain all the time. I appreciate when my mind is in distress, as I want to analyze what is going on with me and catch myself before I act my anguish out in an unproductive or disrespectful manner. But I don't want to be in constant distress, anguish or pain.

It's okay that pain shows us the way; but ultimately, where is that way leading?

To find peace within ourselves, to harness warm, loving feelings generated by doing the right things, to experience joy, to reach inner fulfillment—these things can't happen in a constant state of misery.

Let's say that you did the right things on your self-discovery journey so far; you admitted to and understand your flaws and how these flaws affect others. You expressed remorse, said sorry, asked for forgiveness, did everything in your power to not repeat the same mistakes again and got lots of positive feedback from others acknowledging your change. And yet, you still feel mentally crushed and in pain. You may feel desperate. *I've done everything that I'm supposed to do, I feel like I became the best version of myself. Why do I feel so down still?*

The answer is simple: you didn't forgive yourself.

Often it is much easier to ask for forgiveness and forgive others than to forgive ourselves. In the previous chapter I gave you the exercise to apologize to your own self for the negative self-treatment you practiced. But did you also forgive yourself?

Let's take a look at how an apology works with other

people. We admit the wrongdoing, we acknowledge the anguish we caused, we sincerely repent our actions, we ask permission to make our mistakes right and finally we ask for forgiveness. The other person then may accept or reject our apology. But even if they accept it, some time has to pass for them to be able to sincerely forgive us. There is a space between asking for forgiveness and receiving the forgiveness.

This process is still true when we apologize and seek forgiveness from ourselves. We may need a little time to see how honest we really are, how hard we really try. This is normal. But the longer we delay to grant forgiveness to ourselves, the more we prolong our state of inner discomfort.

At some point we need to forgive ourselves. As Archbishop Desmond Tutu said, "The reasons for forgiving ourselves are the same as for forgiving others. It is how we become free of the past. It is how we heal and grow. It is how we make meaning out of our suffering; restore our self-esteem and tell a new story of who we are."

When we decide to forgive others or seek forgiveness

from others leads to an external peace. When we forgive ourselves leads to an inner peace.

Forgiving ourselves doesn't mean giving ourselves a free pass or letting us off the hook. When we do something bad and then we say, "I stole the job opportunity from my colleague but I forgive myself so all's good."—that is not self-forgiveness. It is a very sinister form of self-excuse that fails to express any remorse, and holds no potential for spiritual growth within. Without remorse and apology there can't be forgiveness.

Self-forgiveness serves the purpose of not punishing ourselves with cruelty, to not take torturous mental revenge on our striving heart. This doesn't mean that when we forgive ourselves we are not still accountable and responsible for the harm we may have caused. We still have to apologize, understand the harm and feel the guilt and remorse that follows such realizations—only then can we move to self-forgiveness with an honest heart.

But we should not skip the part where we forgive ourselves in the healing process and approach restitution from a constructive and non-self-destructive angle. You know, treat yourself as you'd treat a close friend.

There are cases when, as I mentioned before, the conflict is inside us. We were the culprits of the hurt and we are also the victims of it. Negative self-talk, unfulfilled promises we made to ourselves, harsh criticism, the inability to protect our boundaries—these can all create internal tension. *I'm so angry with myself for doing* this *or not doing* that... Do you say this often? What do you usually do when you're angry with yourself? Do you beat your self-esteem to death or do you practice empathy with yourself? Think about it.

However you wronged yourself (skipping the gym, eating fatty food, failing to say no and suffering through an evening with colleagues you don't like), it created internal tension in you. Unless you forgive yourself and let the event go, you won't find peace.

But won't I just excuse myself if I do that? What if forgiving myself for eating a donut today will enable me to eat two tomorrow?

If you do that, it's not self-forgiveness but again, just

an excuse. In order to honestly be able to forgive yourself you need to acknowledge the anguish you caused yourself and commit to not repeat it in the future. Just as you would with a friend. Otherwise you won't find peace; the state of mental pain will persist. Remain honest with yourself. Always—even when you grant self-forgiveness. If you're true in your intentions and strict in your resolution to do your best to stop the wrongdoing, self-forgiveness will grant you that final element you need to finally feel at peace.

Self-forgiveness is a clean slate.

Speaking of clean slates, time to open your journal. On an empty page write down and complete the following statements.

1. **On forgiving myself for hurting others:**

Today I forgive myself for... (name the pain you caused). I sincerely repent for what I did and I acknowledge that my actions affected... (the name of the person you hurt) in this way... (use empathy to express in detail what that other person must have felt).

I am committed to not repeat my hurtful acts and I pledge to correct my mistakes with these actions... (write down at least three things what you'll do to correct the wrong you caused). I know what I did was wrong. I know I'm committed to make it right. I know I have done the right thing so far—I took responsibility and steps to correct my mistakes. May I be at peace now. I forgive you, (Your Name).

1. **On forgiving myself for hurting myself:**

Today I forgive myself for... (name the pain you caused). I sincerely repent for what I did and I acknowledge that my actions affected me in this way... (use self-empathy to express in detail what you felt).

I am committed to not repeat my hurtful acts and I pledge to correct my mistakes with these actions... (write down at least three things you'll do to correct the harm you caused yourself). I know what I did was wrong. I know I'm committed to make it right. I know I have done the right thing so far—I took responsibility and steps to correct my mistakes. May I be at peace now. I forgive you, (Your Name).

Repeat points A and B for as many cases you wish to grant self-forgiveness. If your wrongdoing was grave, you may need to repeat this exercise over and over again.

I'm still struggling to forgive myself in regards to my grandparents. But it's easier to feel less wretched each time I complete this exercise. Every time I can list new things in the 'three things that I do to correct the wrong I caused' section the pain decreases a bit. Following up on my progress of being a more loving, grateful and affectionate partner and child makes me happy, and I'm sure my grandparents are also happy for me. And they forgave me a long time ago.

If you seek self-forgiveness but you couldn't properly apologize for your mistakes from the person because they are deceased or they are otherwise not available, still complete this exercise truthfully and practice corrective actions towards someone else. For example, if you stole money from someone who died, give the equivalent of the stolen money to this person's family, a charity or a beggar. Walk the right path. Don't let self-hatred in your heart. There is always a way out of it.

There is always a way where there is will.

Complimentary Journal for Chapter 3:

a.) Gold in the Dust. Recall the five biggest failures or devastating moments of your life. They can be anything—a death in your family, a break up, a lost job. Choose a few recent events and a few older ones. Think about them for a few moments and answer the following questions:

Failure #1:

----

1. When this event happened I felt...

____

____

____

1. Six months after this event I felt...

____

____

____

____

1. Five years after this event I felt...

____

____

____

____

1. How did this event change my worldview? What did I learn from this event?

Failure #2:

----

1. When this event happened I felt...

----

1. Six months after this event I felt...

____

1. Five years after this event I felt...

____

____

____

____

1. How did this event change my worldview? What did I learn from this event?

____

____

____

____

Failure #3:

____

1. When this event happened I felt...

----

1. Six months after this event I felt...

----

1. Five years after this event I felt...

----

1. How did this event change my worldview? What did I learn from this event?

____

____

____

____

Failure #4:

____

1. When this event happened I felt...

____

____

____

____

1. Six months after this event I felt...

____

____

____

---

1. Five years after this event I felt...

---

1. How did this event change my worldview? What did I learn from this event?

Failure #5:

---

1. When this event happened I felt...

____

____

____

____

1. Six months after this event I felt...

____

____

____

____

1. Five years after this event I felt...

____

____

____

____

1. How did this event change my worldview? What did I learn from this event?

____

____

____

____

(If the painful event you chose is more recent than five years or six months, just answer points 1 (and 2, if applicable) and add the current time distance and feelings you have in relation to the event today.)

b.) Forgive Yourself like Your Life Depends on It

On forgiving myself for hurting others:

#1:

Today I forgive myself for____________________________________ (name the pain you caused). I sincerely repent for what I did and I acknowledge that my actions affected ___________ (the name of the person you hurt) in this way:

____

(use empathy to express in detail what that other person must have felt).

I am committed to not repeat my hurtful acts and I pledge to correct my mistakes with these actions:

(write down at least three things what you'll do to correct the wrong you caused). I know what I did was wrong. I know I'm committed to make it right. I know I have done the right thing so far—I took responsibility and steps to correct my mistakes. May I be at peace now. I forgive you, __________ (Your Name).

#2:

Today I forgive myself for___________________________________ (name the pain you caused). I sincerely repent for what I did and I acknowledge that my actions affected

__________ (the name of the person you hurt) in this way:

____

____

(use empathy to express in detail what that other person must have felt).

I am committed to not repeat my hurtful acts and I pledge to correct my mistakes with these actions:

____

____

____

____

(write down at least three things what you'll do to correct the wrong you caused). I know what I did was wrong. I know I'm committed to make it right. I know I have done the right thing so far—I took responsibility and steps to correct my mistakes. May I be at peace now. I forgive you, __________ (Your Name).

#3:

Today I forgive myself for_________________________________ (name the pain you caused). I sincerely repent for what I did and I acknowledge that my actions affected __________ (the name of the person you hurt) in this way:

____

____

(use empathy to express in detail what that other person must have felt).

I am committed to not repeat my hurtful acts and I pledge to correct my mistakes with these actions:

____

____

____

____

(write down at least three things what you'll do to

correct the wrong you caused). I know what I did was wrong. I know I'm committed to make it right. I know I have done the right thing so far—I took responsibility and steps to correct my mistakes. May I be at peace now. I forgive you, __________ (Your Name).

#4:

Today I forgive myself for__________________________________ (name the pain you caused). I sincerely repent for what I did and I acknowledge that my actions affected __________ (the name of the person you hurt) in this way:

____

____

(use empathy to express in detail what that other person must have felt).

I am committed to not repeat my hurtful acts and I pledge to correct my mistakes with these actions:

____

____

____

____

(write down at least three things what you'll do to correct the wrong you caused). I know what I did was wrong. I know I'm committed to make it right. I know I have done the right thing so far—I took responsibility and steps to correct my mistakes. May I be at peace now. I forgive you, __________ (Your Name).

#5:

Today I forgive myself for________________________________ (name the pain you caused). I sincerely repent for what I did and I acknowledge that my actions affected __________ (the name of the person you hurt) in this way:

____

____

(use empathy to express in detail what that other person must have felt).

I am committed to not repeat my hurtful acts and I pledge to correct my mistakes with these actions:

____

____

____

____

(write down at least three things what you'll do to correct the wrong you caused). I know what I did was wrong. I know I'm committed to make it right. I know I have done the right thing so far—I took responsibility and steps to correct my mistakes. May I be at peace now. I forgive you, __________ (Your Name).

On forgiving myself for hurting myself:

#1:

Today I forgive myself for __________________________________ (name the pain you caused). I sincerely repent for what I did and I acknowledge that my actions affected me in this way:

(use self-empathy to express in detail what you felt).

I am committed to not repeat my hurtful acts and I pledge to correct my mistakes with these actions

----

(write down at least three things you'll do to correct the harm you caused yourself). I know what I did was wrong. I know I'm committed to make it right. I know I have done the right thing so far—I took responsibility and steps to correct my mistakes. May I be at peace now. I forgive you, ______ (Your Name).

#2:

Today I forgive myself for ________________________________ (name the pain you caused). I sincerely repent for what I did and I acknowledge that my actions affected me in this way:

____

____

(use self-empathy to express in detail what you felt).

I am committed to not repeat my hurtful acts and I pledge to correct my mistakes with these actions

____

____

____

____

(write down at least three things you'll do to correct the harm you caused yourself). I know what I did was wrong. I know I'm committed to make it right. I know I have done the right thing so far—I took responsibility and steps to correct my mistakes. May I be at peace now. I forgive you, _____ (Your Name).

#3:

Today I forgive myself for ________________________________ (name the pain you caused). I sincerely repent for what I did and I acknowledge that my actions affected me in this way:

____

____

(use self-empathy to express in detail what you felt).

I am committed to not repeat my hurtful acts and I pledge to correct my mistakes with these actions

____

____

____

____

(write down at least three things you'll do to correct the harm you caused yourself). I know what I did was wrong. I know I'm committed to make it right. I know I have done the right thing so far—I took responsibility and steps to correct my mistakes. May I be at peace now. I forgive you, ______ (Your Name).

#4:

Today I forgive myself for ________________________________ (name the pain you caused). I sincerely repent for what I did and I acknowledge that my actions affected me in this way: _________________________________

____

(use self-empathy to express in detail what you felt).

I am committed to not repeat my hurtful acts and I pledge to correct my mistakes with these actions

____

____

____

____

(write down at least three things you'll do to correct the harm you caused yourself). I know what I did was wrong. I know I'm committed to make it right. I know I have done the right thing so far—I took responsibility and steps to correct my mistakes. May I be at peace now. I forgive you, ______ (Your Name).

#5:

Today I forgive myself for ________________________________ (name the pain you caused). I sincerely repent for what I did and I acknowledge that my actions affected me in this way:

____

____

(use self-empathy to express in detail what you felt).

I am committed to not repeat my hurtful acts and I pledge to correct my mistakes with these actions

____

____

____

____

(write down at least three things you'll do to correct the harm you caused yourself). I know what I did was wrong. I know I'm committed to make it right. I know I have done the right thing so far—I took responsibility and steps to correct my mistakes. May I be at peace now. I forgive you, ______ (Your Name).

4

Step Four: Conscious Transformation

THIS LAST INSTALLMENT OF JOURNALING FOR change, in my opinion, is the most important part.

IN THE FIRST chapter we talked about the signs of emotional immaturity: what they are, how to detect them, how to dig deeper and understand why we are the way we are.

IN THE SECOND chapter we talked about the force that holds back improvement at its core, and that's the force of blaming others and talking down to ourselves. The second chapter gave you an overview on what you shouldn't do—and also what you should focus on when you seek improvement in your behavior and emotional life.

IN THE THIRD chapter I gave you a glimpse of the process of change. I tried my best to not glamourize anything about this process and to keep your expectations regarding your self-improvement journey down to earth. In my opinion there is no easy way, no short way, no painless way—and there shouldn't be. Each step in the process of change is valuable. If one step is missed, the change might not solidify. For example, if we can't attach sufficient pain to our bad behavior, we may never change it.

THESE THREE CHAPTERS came together to prepare you for this final grand step: namely, what is your end goal with this change? What kind of person do you want to be? What skills and attributes do you want to learn or strengthen in yourself? Ultimately, in this chapter I will present the main characteristics of emotional maturity according to Lindsay C. Gibson.

. . .

LET'S START by defining the characteristics of an emotionally mature person. I will present them as present-tense statements.

- I'm able to think objectively and conceptually, channeling a deep emotional connection with others;
- I can function independently while having deep emotional attachments;
- I'm direct in doing what I want but I do this without exploiting others;
- I'm comfortable and honest about my feelings and get along well with others thanks to my well-developed empathy skills, impulse control, and emotional intelligence;
- I'm interested in other people's inner lives, feelings and thoughts. I also enjoy opening up in an emotionally intimate way;
- When I have a problem with someone I face them directly to smooth out our differences;
- I cope with stress in a realistic, forward-looking way while consciously processing my thoughts and feelings;

- I can control my emotions when necessary, adapt to reality and use empathy and humor to strengthen bonds with others;[1]
- I enjoy being objective and know myself well enough to admit my weaknesses;
- I'm comfortable with admitting when I am wrong, taking responsibility for my actions, apologizing and making amends;
- I respect individual differences and that someone else's idea is just as valid from their perspective as mine is from my viewpoint; and
- I know I don't need to agree with someone about their opinion but I can show consideration by accepting that they see something differently

HOW DO you feel about these bullet points? Are the behaviors described in these statements anything you'd like to have? If so, I'd strongly suggest you write the ones that resonate with your ideal self the most in your journal.

. . .

YOU ARE NOT YOUR HABITS. You can choose to change the parts of yourself that you don't like. I'm more sure about this statement than ever. You can reconnect with your authentic self that has adopted unhealthy coping mechanisms in childhood for self-protection. But beneath the many layers of this created, false self lays your true self, your ideal, authentic self that you can rediscover with patience and devotion. One key skill to break through the layers of the false self is self-reflection. Journaling is a great tool to self-reflect.

SPECIFYING our ideal self is harder than it sounds. I hit a roadblock when I tried to self-reflect and define the person who I really, truly, honestly wanted to be (or who I was beneath the surface). After extensive research I understood that, first, I had to deconstruct the lies that I created around my persona even more than before. According to experts like Lindsay C. Gibson, we have two false selves: one that she calls our healing fantasy, the other the role-self. Both of these false selves are adopted in child-hood as defense mechanisms.

. . .

THE HEALING FANTASY develops based on what we thought we needed to feel loved, whole and worthy. As we grow up, we start seeking our healing fantasies in others to repair and fill what we lacked in our childhood. We naturally feel attracted to those who seem to be able to fulfill our healing fantasy.

THE ROLE-SELF IS a cluster of behaviors we adopt to fit in the role we thought our primary caregivers expected from us in order to feel loved. For example, our parents may have withheld love from us when we, as curious children, tried out new things that sometimes were dangerous. Our parents scolded us, didn't give us chocolate, banned us from watching television or even spanked us. We learned that if we are curious, we get in trouble and we get deprived of the things we love. To keep the love of our parents, we adopted a role-self where we behaved as little robots, repressing every spark of curiosity in ourselves. Without being aware of it, this is how we act as adults, too.

GETTING to know these two selves will help you discover your hidden ideas about how other people should treat you so that you feel valued and how you think you must behave to be loved. (In the Journal Mode section I will guide you through the process of identifying your healing fantasy and role-self.) When you uncover these two false selves you'll get a step closer to identifying what those things are that you truly want, instead of what you think you want out of fear of abandonment and inadequacy.

THIS PROCESS IS NOT PAINLESS. As your healing fantasy and role-self are losing legitimacy in your mind, their loss will hurt. You'll feel insecurity and emotional distress. But this means that your true, ideal self is trying to break through your constructed persona, which will become harder and harder to maintain.

AFTER YOU HAVE a clear picture of the adopted parts constructing your healing fantasy and role-self, it's time to make an effort to discover who you really are. When you do this exercise, make sure to avoid words like 'should', 'have to', 'must', 'need', 'supposed to', etc. Also, use affirmations instead of negations. For example, instead of saying, "I don't want to argue anymore," say, "I will solve my problems with a peaceful approach." These are little nuances in thinking but they make a tremendous difference in our changing process.

THERE IS this little moralistic story about an old Cherokee who is teaching his grandson about life:

"A FIGHT IS GOING on inside me," he said to the boy. "It is a terrible fight and it is between two wolves. One is evil—he is anger, envy, sorrow, regret, greed, arrogance, self-pity, guilt, resentment, inferiority, lies, false pride, superiority and ego." He continued, "The other is good—he is joy, peace, love, hope, serenity, humility, kindness, benevolence, empathy, generosity, truth, compassion and faith. The same fight is going on inside you—and inside every other person, too."

THE KID THOUGHT about it for a minute and then asked his grandfather: "Which wolf will win?"

. . .

THE OLD CHEROKEE SIMPLY REPLIED, "The one you feed."

THE MORAL OF this story is that even if we think we are on the road to change our negative habits but we keep our focus on not wanting them, we still think about them. We are not adopting an alternative, good habit but we are fighting the old one. We're feeding the wrong wolf.

IF YOU DON'T FEEL comfortable depending on a fictional quote's wisdom when you plan out your path towards change, I don't blame you. No standalone quote changed my life either. Quotes are good motivators, for sure, but they don't offer a strong enough assurance to take action. You won't say, "I will only make affirmative statements and focus on the positive because the old Cherokee told that to his grandson." Luckily for us, skeptics, there is another source of information that could back quotes such as this one with more evidence. This source of information is science.

. . .

PREVIOUSLY, neuroscientists believed that while a child's brain plasticity was phenomenally capable of change, an adult's brain activity was set in stone. According to early studies of the adult brain, it was said that it could only change due to loss of neurons. There is no regeneration, just degeneration. More recent studies, however, discovered that the old brain studies were simply incorrect. Adult brains can and are indeed changing constantly on a physical level due to our thoughts. Yes, that's correct.

IN HER BOOK *The Intention Experiment* Lynne McTaggart says:

"A SIZABLE BODY of research exploring the nature of consciousness, carried on for more than thirty years in prestigious scientific institutions around the world, shows that thoughts are capable of affecting everything from the simplest machines to the most complex living beings. This evidence suggests that human thoughts and intentions are an actual physical 'something' with astonishing power to change our world. Every thought we have is tangible energy with the power to transform."

. . .

THOUGHTS WE HAVE CREATE neurochemical changes in our brain; some of these are temporary and some long lasting. For example, by consciously practicing gratitude, a certain amount of rewarding neurotransmitters (dopamine and norepinephrine) get released in our body and consequently we will feel better; more positive, alert and joyful.

DR. JOE DISPENZA, a bestselling author and neuroscientist, says that your thoughts also alter your brain in permanent ways. Imagine your mind as a highway of information in your nervous system. On this highway there are many cars (electrical signals) circulating up and down. This is mostly happening unconsciously. Meanwhile thoughts cross your brain; neurons fire together in different ways—depending on the information being handled. These various patterns of neural activity actually change your brain's neural structure over time. Some parts of the brain form new connections with each other. Existing connections between neurons that are more often activated get stronger. Slowly they build more receptors and new neural connections (synapses) are formed.[2]

IF YOU BOMBARD your brain with negative thoughts, you are literally programming your neurons to strengthen the existing negative pathways and to create new ones. Luckily, you can rewrite the existing pathways with new, better pathways you actually wish to have. What can you do to achieve that? Listen to the old Cherokee—and the many scientists who endorse focusing on what you want. Every thought shapes your brain's reality.

Journal Mode

1. What kind of person do I want to be?

At the top of a blank sheet in your journal write down 'My Ideal Self'. Under this caption write down every bullet point you want to adopt from the beginning of this chapter. (Remember, these are the characteristics of an emotionally mature person.) After you're done with the given characteristics, come up with at least five more behaviors you'd like to adopt. (Not 'leave behind' but 'adopt'; focus on what you want.)

2. Discover your healing fantasy.

On a blank sheet of your journal write down

'Healing Fantasy' and fill in the gaps of the following statements honestly. Don't ponder for too long on what to answer, just write down whatever instantly comes into your mind after reading the statement.

1. I wish other people were more...
2. Why is it so hard for people to...
3. I would like someone to treat me like...
4. Maybe one of these days I will find someone who will...
5. In an ideal world with good people, others would...[1]

3. Discover your role-self.

On a blank sheet in your journal write down 'Role-Self' and fill in the gaps of the following statements honestly. Don't ponder for too long on what to answer, just write down whatever instantly comes into your mind after reading the statement.

1. I try hard to be...
2. The main reason people like me is because...
3. Other people don't appreciate how much I...

4. I always have to be the one who...
5. I've tried to be the kind of person who...

4. Your ideal self.

On a blank sheet in your journal write down 'Ideal Self' and list at least ten positive affirmations about the person who you'd like to be.

- Remember, focus on what you want to do, not on what you want to avoid or overcome;
- For example, "I want to say kind words to my partner." Not: "I don't want to be mean to my partner."
- Phrase your positive affirmations in the present tense;
- For example, "I'm a kind partner." Not: "I wish I will be more kind with my partner."
- Don't use words like 'should', 'have to', 'must', 'need' or 'supposed to';
- For example, "I'm grateful for what I have." Not: "I should be more grateful for what I have."
- Try to avoid definitive words like 'always', 'never', 'all the time' or 'every time';
- For example, say, "I'm a happy, fulfilled

person." Not: "I want to be always happy and fulfilled."

- Be as specific as you can about what you want
- For example, "I spend more time with my children, listen more deeply about what they have to say and I do my best to put myself in their shoes." Not: "I want to be a better mother."

I'm sure these bullet points seem overly restrictive at first. *Isn't it enough that I have to come up with ten things? Do I need to nail more aspects of them than of a fine prose?*

There is a reason why I helped you with these guiding points. Using them in the creation of your ideal self will make the entire process of change easier. These points are also endorsed by great self-development experts like Tony Robbins—keep yourself in the present, be focused, keep your goal realistic and give yourself a specific direction.

I won't rush you with this exercise; take as much time as you want or need. This entire book has built up to this moment, it was written to complete this exercise

—and of course to start acting on it once it is completed.

Complimentary Journal for Chapter 4:

a.) The characteristics of an emotionally mature person presented as present-tense statements. Which of these attributives do you have or would you like to adopt?

- I'm able to think objectively and conceptually, channeling a deep emotional connection with others; ____
- I can function independently while having deep emotional attachments; ____
- I'm direct in doing what I want but I do this without exploiting others; ____
- I'm comfortable and honest about my feelings and get along well with others thanks to my well-developed empathy

skills, impulse control, and emotional intelligence; ____

- I'm interested in other people's inner lives, feelings and thoughts. I also enjoy opening up in an emotionally intimate way; ____
- When I have a problem with someone I face them directly to smooth out our differences; ____
- I cope with stress in a realistic, forward-looking way while consciously processing my thoughts and feelings; ____
- I can control my emotions when necessary, adapt to reality and use empathy and humor to strengthen bonds with others;[1]

  ____
- I enjoy being objective and know myself well enough to admit my weaknesses; ____
- I'm comfortable with admitting when I am wrong, taking responsibility for my actions, apologizing and making amends; ____
- I respect individual differences and that someone else's idea is just as valid from their perspective as mine is from my viewpoint; ____
- I know I don't need to agree with someone about their opinion but I can show

consideration by accepting that they see something differently. ____

b.) What kind of person do I want to be? What's my ideal self?

Write down every bullet point you want to adopt from point a.). Then come up with at least five more behaviors you'd like to adopt. Remember, not 'leave behind' but 'adopt'; focus on what you want.

- Remember, focus on what you want to do, not on what you want to avoid or overcome;

- Phrase your positive affirmations in the present tense;

- Don't use words like 'should', 'have to', 'must', 'need' or 'supposed to';

- Try to avoid definitive words like 'always', 'never', 'all the time' or 'every time';

- Be as specific as you can about what you want

My Ideal Self

____

____

____

____

____

____

____

____

____

____

____

____

____

____

My Healing Fantasy

(Don't ponder for too long on what to answer, just write down whatever instantly comes into your mind after reading the statement.)

"I wish other people were more...

____

____

____

____

____

____

Why is it so hard for people to...

____

____

____

____

____

____

I would like someone to treat me like...

____

____

____

____

____

____

Maybe one of these days I will find someone who will...

____

____

____

____

____

____

In an ideal world with good people, others would..."[1]

____

____

____

____

____

____

My Role Self

(Don't ponder for too long on what to answer, just write down whatever instantly comes into your mind after reading the statement.)

"I try hard to be...

____

The main reason people like me is because...

____

____

____

____

____

____

Other people don't appreciate how much I...

____

____

____

____

____

____

I always have to be the one who...

I've tried to be the kind of person who..."

Don't rush you with this exercise; take as much time as you want. The book and journal have built up to this moment; they were written to complete these exercises —and of course to start or stop acting on them once they are completed.

Final Words

Thank you for being with me on the short journey this book took you through. Your longer journey is just about to start. I really hope I was able to give you some insights and shortcut your struggles a little bit with a few good tips regarding self-understanding through journaling. There is nothing in this book that I haven't done myself in the past few months; and there is nothing written that I have done and didn't help. God knows I didn't put every single dead-end street of my change journey in here—only the tested and working ones.

The thoughts, books and journaling practices shared in this book helped me a lot. They might not work for you the same way they worked their magic on me, so feel free to play around with the information and make changes to fit your personality. Some of my steps, however, are universal. What are these steps?

- Without awareness and the ability to self-reflect, conscious change is impossible;
- Change doesn't happen overnight and it's not easy;
- Blaming others and being overly harsh to yourself won't make you a better person; and
- In order to change into the person you'd like to be, first you need to know crystal clear what that person looks like

The rest of the information I presented in this book is the 'how-to' part for these four crucial bullet points. Make sure you nail these four with the help of my tips or with your own and enjoy the liberating feeling of being your true self.

"The true self seeks release, not constraint. It doesn't want to be corseted in a sonnet or made to learn a system of musical notations. It wants liberation, which is why very often it fastens on the novel, for the novel seems spacious, undefined, free."

- By Rachel Cusk

Seek the novel, my friend. Open up and own your beautiful soul with serenity and pride, with the gentle touch of a strong heart, with the ever-changing state of hope and hopelessness of being a lovable and flawed human being.

I love you.

Zoe

Are You Still With Me?

Thank you so much for choosing to read my book among the many out there. I know your time is valuable and you chose to share it with me. I deeply appreciate you for this.

How did you like Think Different? Would you consider leaving a review about your reading experience so other readers could know about it? If you are willing to give a little more of your time to do so, there are several options:

1. Leave a review on Amazon https://www.amazon.com/review/create-review?asin=B07NP4D9RS#

2. Leave a review on goodreads.com. Here is a link to my profile (https://www.goodreads.com/author/show/14967542.Zoe_McKey)where you can find all of my books. You can also follow my 2019 Reading Challenge. I proposed the ambitious goal of reading 100 books in 2019. Find the list of the books I'm reading/read on my GoodReads profile;
3. Send me an email to zoemckey@gmail.com; and
4. Tell your friends and family about your reading experience

Your feedback is very important and valuable to me. It helps me assess if I'm on the right path providing help to you and where I need to improve. Your feedback is also valuable to other people as they can learn about my work and perhaps give an independent author such as myself a chance. I deeply appreciate any kind of feedback you take the time to provide me.

If you'd like to receive an update once I have a new book, you can subscribe to my newsletter at www.zoemckey.com. You'll get a My Daily Routine Makeover cheat sheet and an Unbreakable Confidence checklist for FREE. You'll also get occasional book recommendations from other authors I trust.

Other Books by Zoe McKey

Brave Enough

Time to learn how to overcome the feeling of inferiority and achieve success. Brave Enough takes you step by step through the process of understanding the nature of your fears, overcome limiting beliefs and gain confidence with the help of studies, personal stories and actionable exercises at the end of each chapter.

Say goodbye to a fear of rejection and an inferiority complex once and for all.

Daily Habit Makeover

The time to do something about your bad habits is right now —otherwise, you are in danger of never starting. Learn to identify, prioritize and focus on your most important tasks and get them done.

Unlearn bad habits and build powerful, helpful ones.

Less Mess Less Stress

Don't compromise with your happiness. "Good enough" is not the life you deserve—you deserve the best, and the good news is that you can have it. Learn the surprising truth that it's not by doing more, but less with Less Mess Less Stress.

We know that we own too much, that we say yes to too many engagements and that we stick to more than we should. Physical, mental and relationship clutter are daily burdens we have to deal with. Change your mindset and live a happier life with less.

Minimalist Budget

Minimalist Budget will help you turn your bloated expenses into a well-toned budget, spending on exactly what you need and nothing else.

This book presents solutions for two major problems in our consumer society: (1) how to downsize your cravings without having to sacrifice the fun stuff, and (2) how to whip your finances into shape and follow a personalized budget.

Rewire Your Habits

Rewire Your Habits discusses which habits one should adopt to make changes in 5 life areas: self-improvement, relationships, money management, health and free time.

The book addresses every goal-setting, habit-building challenge in these areas and breaks them down with simplicity and ease.

Tame Your Emotions

Tame Your Emotions is a collection of the most common and painful emotional insecurities and their antidotes. Even the most successful people have fears and self-sabotaging habits. But they also know how to use them to their advantage and keep their fears on a short leash. This is exactly what my book will teach you—using the tactics of experts and research-proven methods.

Emotions can't be eradicated. But they can be controlled.

The Art of Minimalism

The Art of Minimalism will present you 4 minimalist techniques, the best from around the world, to give you a perspective on how to declutter your house, your mind and your life in general. Learn how to let go of everything that is not important in your life and find methods that give you peace of mind and happiness instead.

Keep balance at the edge of minimalism and consumerism.

The Critical Mind

If you want to become a critical, effective and rational thinker instead of an irrational and snap-judging one, this book is for you. Critical thinking skills strengthen your decision-making muscle, speed up your analysis and judgment and help you spot errors easily.

The Critical Mind offers a thorough introduction to the rules and principles of critical thinking. You will find widely usable and situation-specific advice on how to critically approach your daily life, business, friendships, opinions and even social media.

The Disciplined Mind

Where you end up in life is determined by the number of times you fall and get up, and how much pain and discomfort you can withstand along the way. The path to an extraordinary accomplishment and a life worth living is not innate talent, but focus, willpower and disciplined action.

Maximize your brain power and keep control of your thoughts.

In The Disciplined Mind, you will find unique lessons through which you will learn those essential steps and qualities that are needed to reach your goals easier and faster.

The Unlimited Mind

This book collects all the tips, tricks and tactics of the most successful people to develop your inner smartness.

The Unlimited Mind will show you how to think smarter and find your inner genius. This book is a collection of research and scientific studies about better decision-making, fairer judgments and intuition improvement. It takes a critical look at our everyday cognitive habits and points out small but serious mistakes that are easily correctable.

Who You Were Meant To Be

Discover the strengths of your personality and how to use them to make better life choices. In Who You Were Meant To Be, you'll learn some of the most influential personality-related studies. Thanks to these studies you'll learn to capitalize on your strengths, and how you can become the best version of yourself.

Wired For Confidence

Do you feel like you just aren't good enough? End this vicious thought cycle NOW. Wired For Confidence tells you the necessary steps to break out from the pits of low self-esteem, lowered expectations and lack of assertiveness.

Take the first step to creating the life you only dared to dream of.

To access the full list of my books visit this link.

References

Brant, Andrea. Four Ways Childhood Trauma Impacts Adults. Psychology Today. 2017. https://www.psychologytoday.com/us/blog/mindful-anger/201706/4-ways-childhood-trauma-impacts-adults

Brown, Brene. Rising Strong. Random House Trade Paperbacks. 2017.

Brown, Brene. The Power of Vulnerability. Sounds True. 2013.

Burman, J. T. Jean Piaget: Images of a life and his factory. History of Psychology. 15 (3): 283–288. doi:10.1037/a0025930. ISSN 1093-4510. 2012.

Chapman, Gary. Thomas, Jenifer. When Sorry Isn't Enough. Northfield Publishing. 2013.

Dabrowski, Kazimierz. Personality-Shaping Through Positive Disintegration. Red Pill Press. 2015.

Dispenza, Joe. Dr. Breaking The Habit of Being Yourself. Hay House Inc. 2012.

Duhigg, Charles. The Power of Habit. Cornerstone Digital. 2012.

Gibson, Lindsay C. Adult Children of Emotionally Immature Parents. New Harbinger Publications. 2015.

Hendrix, Harville. Ph.D. Getting The Love You Want. Henry Holt & Co. 2007.

ISixSigma. Determine the root cause: 5 Whys. ISix-Sigma. 2019. https://www.isixsigma.com/tools-templates/cause-effect/determine-root-cause-5-whys/

Kahneman, Daniel. Thinking, fast and slow. Farrar, Straus and Giroux. 2011.

Tutu, Desmond. The Book of Forgiving. William Collins. 2014.

Notes

1. Step One: Awareness

1. Gibson, Lindsay C. Adult Children of Emotionally Immature Parents. New Harbinger Publications. 2015.
2. Duhigg, Charles. The Power of Habit. Cornerstone Digital. 2012.
3. Brown, Brene. Rising Strong. Random House Trade Paperbacks. 2017.
4. Brant, Andrea. Four Ways Childhood Trauma Impacts Adults. Psychology Today. 2017. https://www.psychologytoday.com/us/blog/mindful-anger/201706/4-ways-childhood-trauma-impacts-adults
5. Tutu, Desmond. The Book of Forgiving. William Collins. 2014.
6. Chapman, Gary. Thomas, Jenifer. When Sorry Isn't Enough. Northfield Publishing. 2013.

Journal Mode

1. ISixSigma. Determine the root cause: 5 Whys. ISixSigma. 2019. https://www.isixsigma.com/tools-templates/cause-effect/determine-root-cause-5-whys/

Complimentary Journal for Chapter 1:

1. Gibson, Lindsay C. Adult Children of Emotionally Immature Parents. New Harbinger Publications. 2015.

2. Step Two: Stop the Blame Game

1. Brown, Brene. The Power of Vulnerability. Sounds True. 2013.
2. Kahneman, Daniel. Thinking, fast and slow. Farrar, Straus and Giroux. 2011.

3. Step Three: Forged in Pain

1. Hendrix, Harville. Ph.D. Getting The Love You Want. Henry Holt & Co. 2007.

Journal Mode

1. Burman, J. T. Jean Piaget: Images of a life and his factory. History of Psychology. 15 (3): 283–288. doi:10.1037/a0025930. ISSN 1093-4510. 2012.
2. Dabrowski, Kazimierz. Personality-Shaping Through Positive Disintegration. Red Pill Press. 2015.

4. Step Four: Conscious Transformation

1. Gibson, Lindsay C. Adult Children of Emotionally Immature Parents. New Harbinger Publications. 2015.
2. Dispenza, Joe. Dr. Breaking The Habit of Being Yourself. Hay House Inc. 2012.

Journal Mode

1. Gibson, Lindsay C. Adult Children of Emotionally Immature Parents. New Harbinger Publications. 2015.

Complimentary Journal for Chapter 4:

1. Gibson, Lindsay C. Adult Children of Emotionally Immature Parents. New Harbinger Publications. 2015.

My Healing Fantasy

1. Gibson, Lindsay C. Adult Children of Emotionally Immature Parents. New Harbinger Publications. 2015.